Britannica's

WORD of the DAY

Britannica Books is an imprint of What on Earth Publishing,
published in collaboration with Britannica, Inc.
The Black Barn, Wickhurst Farm, Tonbridge, Kent TN11 8PS, United Kingdom
30 Ridge Road Unit B, Greenbelt, Maryland, 20770, United States

First published in the United Kingdom in 2022

Contributors
Cover illustration by Josy Bloggs
Interior illustrations by Josy Bloggs, Emily Cox, James Gibbs and Liz Kay
For a detailed list of illustration credits, please see p.353.
Text by Patrick Kelly, Renee Kelly and Sue Macy
Designed by Daisy Symes
Editing of 2021 edition by Max Bisantz
Editing of UK edition by Helen Szirtes
Book production and print production by Booklabs.co.uk

Encyclopaedia Britannica
Alison Eldridge, Managing Editor; Michele Rita Metych, Fact Checker

Britannica Books
Nancy Feresten, Publisher; Natalie Bellos, Executive Editor; Meg Osborne, Assistant Editor; Andy Forshaw, Art Director; Daisy Symes, Designer

A CIP catalogue record for this book is available from the British Library
ISBN: 9781913750350
Printed in China | DC/Foshan, China/04/2024

10 9 8 7 6 5 4 3 2

whatonearthbooks.com

Britannica's

WORD of the DAY

••••••••••••••••••

366 Elevating Utterances to Stretch Your Cranium and Tickle Your Humerus

Jan

uary

1 JANUARY

Razzmatazz

(raz-muh-TAZ)

noisy and exciting activity meant to attract attention (noun)

Circus performers blend athletic skills with the *razzmatazz* of show business. Dressed in colourful costumes, they perform acrobatics and balancing routines under bright lights as music blares and fans watch in wonder.

2 JANUARY

Hoodwink

(HOOD-wink)

to trick or deceive (verb)

Frank Abagnale was an American conman in the 1960s who tricked banks, businesses and people into giving him money and power. At age 16, he managed to *hoodwink* an airline company into believing he was a pilot by wearing a pilot's uniform and making a fake licence.

3 JANUARY

Proverbial

(pruh-VER-bee-uhl)

of, relating to or resembling a proverb (adjective)

A proverb is a saying that offers advice or a common truth. The proverb ‘curiosity killed the cat’ suggests that too much curiosity could get a person into trouble. Even without whiskers and a tail, a curious person could be called the *proverbial* cat.

4 JANUARY

Ovation

(oh-VAY-shuhn)

an expression of approval or enthusiasm made by clapping or cheering (noun)

Spanish opera star Placido Domingo is thought to hold the record for receiving the longest standing *ovation* in history. It took place after a 1991 performance of Verdi's *Otello* in Vienna and lasted 80 minutes. The singer took his curtain call, the part where the performer comes to the front of the stage to receive applause, 101 times.

5 JANUARY

Guffaw

(guh-FAW)

a loud and hearty laugh (noun)

When people laugh, their bodies are producing a strong physical reaction. For a small giggle, the vocal cords vibrate. For a good laugh, like a *guffaw*, air is pushed out of the lungs so fast that the rib and belly muscles spasm.

6 JANUARY

Epiphany

(ih-PIF-uh-nee)

a sudden understanding or realisation of something in a new or very clear way (noun)

When asked to define an *epiphany*, poet Maya Angelou said, ‘It’s the occurrence when the mind, the body, the heart and the soul focus together and see an old thing in a new way.’

7 JANUARY

Ad-lib

(AD-LIB)

to make up something on the spot without planning, especially music or spoken words during a performance (verb)

Rappers and comedians are famous for *ad-libbing*, but sometimes actors go off script too. In *Avengers: Infinity War*, Chadwick Boseman and Winston Duke (Black Panther and M'Baku) ad-libbed the war chants at the start of the battle against Thanos. It became one of the most iconic moments in the movie.

8 JANUARY

Klutz

(KLUTS)

a clumsy person (noun)

In 2020, a *klutz* in an Italian museum tried to take a selfie and ended up tripping and falling into a 200-year-old statue by sculptor Antonio Canova, snapping off a few of the statue's toes.

Disaster!

When things get out of hand, these words come into play.

10 JANUARY

Fiasco

(fee-ASK-oh)

a complete failure (noun)

The 2014 Sochi Winter Olympics in Russia almost turned into a *fiasco* when unseasonably warm weather melted the snow and caused snowboarders and ski jumpers to fall while competing.

9 JANUARY

Mayhem

(MAY-hem)

a situation with little order or control, or unnecessary destruction (noun)

Scenes of *mayhem* take place in cities across the world on International Pillow Fight Day. Flash mobs are organised online, and anyone can turn up with a pillow as long as they wield it responsibly.

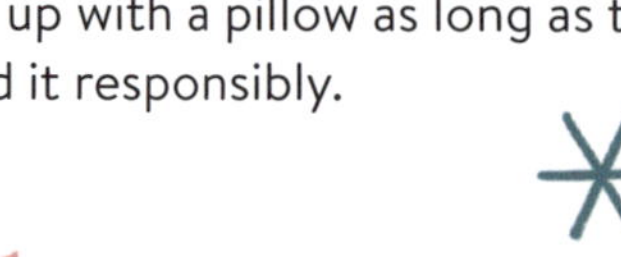

11 JANUARY

Smithereens

(smih-thuh-REENZ)

small broken pieces (plural noun)

A stained-glass window in Christchurch, New Zealand, was smashed to *smithereens* during a 2010 earthquake. It took 18 months to put the window back together.

12 JANUARY

Pandemonium

(pan-duh-MOH-nee-uhm)

a wild uproar (noun)

There was *pandemonium* at the 2005 Glastonbury music festival, when heavy rains caused the electricity to go out, tents to flood and portable toilets to sink into the mud.

13 JANUARY

Hazmat

(HAZ-mat)

a substance that poses a risk to people's health or to the environment (noun). Hazmat comes from *hazardous* material.

When an oil spill occurred off the coast of Thailand in 2013, members of Thailand's military wore *hazmat* suits to clean up the black sludge from the country's beaches.

14 JANUARY

Zany

(ZAY-nee)

very strange and silly (adjective)

Early 20th-century Swiss clown Charles Adrien Wettach, better known as Grock, is often called 'The King of Clowns'. While most clowns of his era performed outside, Wettach performed his *zany* comedy, musical and acrobatics routines inside royal concert halls for elite crowds.

15 JANUARY

Rectify

(REK-tuh-fye)

to correct or make right (verb)

In 2012, an elderly parishioner became concerned that a portrait of Jesus Christ in her church in Borja, Spain, was being damaged by a leak. She decided to *rectify* the situation by restoring the painting herself. At first locals were shocked by her botched attempt, but the fresco soon became an internet sensation, bringing in thousands of tourists.

16 JANUARY

Cadre

(KAHD-ruh)

a group of people working closely together for a purpose (noun)

In 1943, an international *cadre* of soldiers and civilians known as 'The Monuments Men' were tasked with protecting historic art from destruction during World War II. They shipped important art out of harm's way so it could be enjoyed for generations to come.

17 JANUARY

Dumbfounded

(DUM-fown-did)

very shocked or surprised (adjective)

When the New Zealand singer Lorde won two Grammy Awards for her song 'Royals' in 2014, her mother told a radio station, 'As a mum, when I sat there, I was in shock. You feel a bit *dumbfounded* when you hear your daughter's name called out amongst such company.'

18 JANUARY

Tomfoolery

(tom-FOO-luh-ree)

playful or foolish behaviour (noun)

In her book *Anne of Green Gables*, author Lucy Maud Montgomery had one character describe Anne as 'writing stories or practising dialogues or some such *tomfoolery*, and never thinking once about the time or her duties'. That grumpy character obviously didn't think writing or acting was serious work!

19 JANUARY

Virtuoso

(ver-choo-OH-soh)

a person who is an outstanding performer, especially in music (noun)

Singer-songwriter Prince, born in 1958, was considered a *virtuoso* on guitar, as well as one of the greatest musicians of his generation.

20 JANUARY

Quibble

(KWIB-uhl)

to argue or complain about small, unimportant things (verb)

If your friend enjoys a letter you wrote but complains about your handwriting, she probably likes to *quibble*!

21 JANUARY

Satchel

(SATCH-uhl)

a shoulder bag with a long strap, usually made of leather (noun)

Although *satchels* are often used to carry laptop computers and tablets today, they have been around for centuries. In his comedy *As You Like It*, William Shakespeare describes a 'schoolboy with his satchel' heading to school.

Where in the World?

Some words come from the names of places that are part of their history. You might be surprised how far some words have travelled.

23 JANUARY

Cheddar

(CHED-er)

a hard white, yellow or orange cheese with flavour ranging from mild to sharp (noun)

Cheddar was first made in the English village of Cheddar.

22 JANUARY

Cantaloupe

(KAN-tuh-loop)

a small melon with rough skin and sweet orange fruit (noun)

Some of the first *cantaloupes* in Europe grew in Cantalupo, Italy.

24 JANUARY

Denim

(DEN-im)

sturdy cotton fabric used to make jeans and other clothing (noun)

Denim was first made in Nimes, France. The French phrase 'de Nimes' means 'from Nimes'.

25 JANUARY

Frankfurter

(FRANK-fer-tuh)

a cooked, smoked sausage, also known as a hot dog (noun)

It is commonly believed that the first *frankfurter* was made in Frankfurt am Main, Germany.

26 JANUARY

Satin

(SAT-in)

a fabric that has a smooth, shiny surface and a dull back (noun)

Traders in the Middle Ages often exported satin from the port city of Quanzhou, China. The name of this fabric probably comes from the Arabic word *zaytūnī*, meaning 'of Zaytūn' – Quanzhou's former name.

27 JANUARY

Tuxedo

(tuk-SEE-doh)

a usually black formal suit worn with a white shirt and a black bow tie (noun)

The *tuxedo* was first worn in the United States at dinner parties of the wealthy in Tuxedo Park, New York.

28 JANUARY

Magnify

(MAG-nih-fye)

to make something appear larger or more important (verb)

Historians believe that British philosopher Roger Bacon created the first magnifying glass for scientific purposes in the Middle Ages. This tool allowed scientists to *magnify* plants, animals and insects to many times their original size.

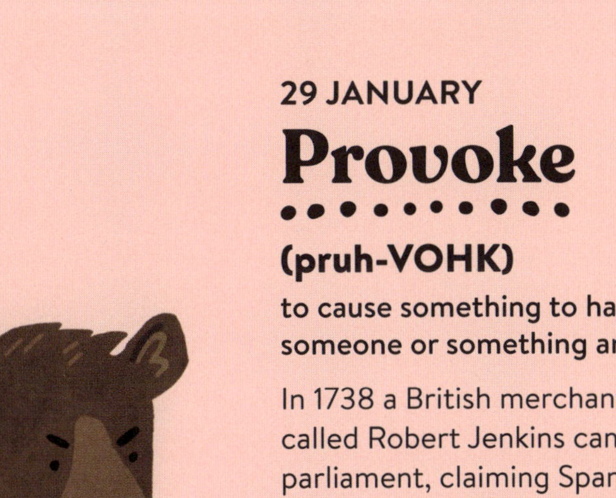

29 JANUARY

Provoke

(pruh-VOHK)

to cause something to happen or make someone or something angry (verb)

In 1738 a British merchant navy captain called Robert Jenkins came before parliament, claiming Spanish coastguards in the West Indies had cut off his ear seven years earlier. Some accounts say he presented the ear in a bottle. His speech caused outrage and *provoked* the War of Jenkins' Ear, which rumbled on until 1748.

30 JANUARY

Hubbub

(HUB-ub)

confusion, uproar (noun)

In the 1943 Looney Tunes cartoon, 'Falling Hare', Bugs Bunny is enjoying a book when he suddenly hears a loud clanging sound. Bugs follows the noise to find a gremlin banging on a piece of metal with a mallet and says, 'What's all the *hubbub*, bub?'

31 JANUARY

Marvel

(MAR-vuhl)

to feel great surprise, wonder or admiration (verb)

In 1939, a company known as Timely Comics published Marvel Comics #1, about an android called The Human Torch. It was the beginning of what would become the fictional Marvel Universe, filled with superheroes readers and viewers would *marvel* at for generations to come.

Story of the Month

I had an ***epiphany*** the other day. My little brother is a ***klutz***. I was ***dumbfounded*** as I watched him attempt a magic trick in front of a ***cadre*** of friends. There he was, in his ***satin tuxedo***, trying to turn a ***cheddar***-wrapped ***frankfurter*** into a ***cantaloupe***. The trick was a ***fiasco***. The cantaloupe, hidden in a ***satchel*** under his jacket, fell to the floor and was smashed to ***smithereens***. I couldn't help but ***guffaw***. My poor brother froze onstage like a ***proverbial*** deer in the headlights.

For his next trick, my brother tried to ***hoodwink*** his friends into thinking he could disappear. I wouldn't ***quibble*** if the trick had worked, but instead, my brother released a smoke bomb and hid behind an old trunk. Overall, my brother's magic show was far from the performance of a ***virtuoso***, and his ***tomfoolery provoked*** quite a ***hubbub*** in the room. Rather than ***ad-lib*** a clever excuse, he tried to cover up his failures with a lot of ***razzmatazz***. He even attempted another trick to ***rectify*** the situation, but that just ended in more ***mayhem***. It was complete ***pandemonium***!

Even so, his friends gave him a standing ***ovation*** for his ***zany*** performance. I have to ***marvel*** at their support, but I worry that their reaction will only ***magnify*** his confidence and encourage him to try again. If he does, I might have to show up wearing a ***hazmat*** suit over my ***denim***!

Febr

uary

1 FEBRUARY

Fusspot

(FUSS-pot)

a person who worries or complains about small things (noun)

Lucy Van Pelt, the leading lady of Charles Schulz's *Peanuts* comic strip, is a *fusspot* who complains about everything. In one comic strip, Lucy complains that her brother, Linus, makes too much noise. When she finds him making a sandwich, Linus asks, 'Am I buttering too loud for you?'

2 FEBRUARY

Yelp

•••••

(YELP)

to make a quick, high-pitched bark or cry, especially of pain or alarm (verb)

Dogs *yelp* for any number of reasons. They may be seeking attention to play or be fed. Or something may have alarmed them. They may even just be over-excited. If they yelp when being touched, they may be expressing pain. In that case, a vet can help distinguish the good yelps from the bad.

3 FEBRUARY

Potholing

(POT-hoh-ling)

the hobby or practice of exploring caves (noun)

There are actually two different words to describe cave exploration. Caving usually refers to cave exploration in a group and mainly involves horizontal passages. Potholing involves descending vertically into caves using ropes and special equipment.

4 FEBRUARY

Delusion

(dih-LOO-zhuhn)

something that is falsely believed to be true despite evidence to the contrary (noun)

In the Middle Ages, many royals suffered from what is now called the glass *delusion*. King Charles VI of France believed his entire body was made of glass and even had special clothing made to 'protect' his delicate organs.

5 FEBRUARY

Woebegone

• • • • • • • • • • • • • •

(WOH-bih-gon)

exhibiting great woe, sorrow or misery (adjective)

People who are paid to cry at funerals, called 'sobbers' or 'professional mourners', have existed since the dawn of time and can be found in ancient Egyptian, Roman and Chinese texts. In ancient Rome, professional mourners were women who would put on a *woebegone* performance, crying loudly and tearing at their hair.

6 FEBRUARY

Grapple

(GRAP-uhl)

to deal with by wrestling, or as if by wrestling (verb)

The word *grapple* can be used both for physical wrestling and for figurative wrestling, such as with a difficult maths problem or other life situation. In the sports of wrestling and mixed martial arts, opponents grapple with one another in hand-to-hand combat, forcing their competitors to the ground.

7 FEBRUARY

Punctual

(PUNK-chuh-wul)

arriving or doing something at the expected or planned time (adjective)

In the animated Disney classic *Cinderella*, Cinderella's fairy godmother provides her with a magical carriage, royal footmen, a ball gown and glass slippers to attend the prince's ball. However, she warns Cinderella to be *punctual*. Cinderella must leave the party before midnight, when the magic will disappear!

8 FEBRUARY

Incorrigible

(in-KOR-ih-jih-buhl)

not able to be corrected or changed (adjective)

Assistance dogs train for years and pass a series of tests to ensure they can do work and perform tasks for a person with a disability. *Incorrigible* dogs who fail these tests by chasing squirrels or pulling on the lead are often put up for adoption to be raised as pets.

9 FEBRUARY

Oodles

• • • • • • • • •

(OO-dulz)

a large amount of something (noun)

In autumn, squirrels and other small animals gather *oodles* of nuts and seeds and hide them away underground. When winter comes, they use their memory and sense of smell to find the buried meals. What happens to the seeds they miss? Some of them sprout into saplings in the spring.

10 FEBRUARY

Sabotage

(SAB-uh-tahzh)

to deliberately obstruct or destroy something (verb)

In wartime, military forces *sabotage* crucial structures such as factories, airports, railways and bridges to hinder their enemy's ability to fight. During World War I, British troops cut German undersea telegram lines to stop communication.

11 FEBRUARY

Dilapidated

(dih-LAP-ih-day-tihd)

falling apart because of age or lack of care (adjective)

In the 1800s, the discovery of gold in California, USA, brought thousands of people to the town of Bodie in hopes of becoming rich. Today, Bodie is an abandoned ghost town turned tourist attraction where visitors can look at the *dilapidated* buildings and get a glimpse of the past.

12 FEBRUARY

Tandem

(TAN-dum)

consisting of two things or having two parts arranged one behind the other (adjective)

When *tandem* bicycles went into production in the 1890s, they were advertised as 'courting bicycles', because couples could pedal together (in tandem), one seated behind the other. This type of bicycle was popularised in the song 'Daisy Bell' as 'a bicycle built for two'.

Love Language

Love is in the air this month. Do any of these lovely words describe you?

13 FEBRUARY

Ailurophile

(eye-LOOR-uh-fyle)

a person who loves cats (noun)

Florence Nightingale, the founder of modern nursing, was also a passionate *ailurophile* who cared for more than 60 cats in her lifetime.

14 FEBRUARY

Bibliophile

(BIB-lee-uh-fyle)

a person who loves or collects books (noun)

Ptolemy II was a pharaoh in ancient Egypt and a noted *bibliophile*. He helped establish the Library of Alexandria, which boasted the largest collection of books in the ancient world until it burned to the ground.

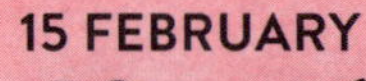

15 FEBRUARY

Cinephile

(SIN-uh-fyle)

a person who loves films (noun)

Cinephiles around the world flock to the Melbourne Museum in Australia to view films on a 32-metre x 23-metre projection screen – one of the biggest in the world.

16 FEBRUARY

Logophile

(LOG-uh-fyle)

a person who loves words (noun)

If you weren't a *logophile* when you started this book, we hope you are by the time you've finished!

17 FEBRUARY

Mycophile

(MYE-koh-fyle)

a person who loves hunting for or eating mushrooms (noun)

It can be hard to tell the difference between edible and poisonous fungi, so foraging *mycophiles* really have to know their straw mushrooms from their death caps.

18 FEBRUARY

Turophile

(TUR-uh-fyle)

a person who loves or is an expert on cheese (noun)

Some *turophiles* turn their passion into a career as a cheesemonger, using their experience and appreciation of their favourite food to sell it to other people.

19 FEBRUARY

Aplomb

(uh-PLOM)

confidence and skill shown, especially in a difficult situation (noun)

In 2021, at the age of 13, Japan's Momiji Nishiya became the second youngest gold medallist in Olympic history. Keeping a cool head in the street skateboarding competition, she landed her final three tricks with *aplomb*, nudging Brazilian Rayssa Leal, Nishiya's junior by a few months, into silver medal position.

20 FEBRUARY

Wanderlust

(WOHN-duh-lust)

a strong desire to travel (noun)

Audrey Walsworth is one of an elite group of women who have visited every country and territory in the world. More people have been into space than have achieved this feat. She discovered her *wanderlust* after her first trip to Lithuania in 1969, and in the fifty years since she has not stopped travelling.

21 FEBRUARY

Mastermind

(MAH-stuh-mynde)

a person who plans and organises something (noun)

In the 1970s and 1980s, rap music was mostly performed live. Sylvia Robinson, a singer and record producer, was the *mastermind* who decided to record a rap song in a studio for listeners across the world. The record, called 'Rapper's Delight', was released in 1979 and was inducted into the Grammy Hall of Fame in 2014.

22 FEBRUARY

Docile

(DOH-sighl)

easily taught, led or controlled (adjective)

In *Frankenstein* by Mary Wollstonecraft Shelley, the monster reassures his creator of his loyalty by saying, 'I am thy creature, and I will be even mild and *docile*.'

23 FEBRUARY

Collaborate

(kuh-LAB-uh-rayt)

to work jointly with others (verb)

Some scientists believe that Albert Einstein and his first wife, Mileva Marić, *collaborated* on his famous equation, $E = mc^2$. Einstein reportedly told a group of intellectuals, 'I need my wife. She solves for me all my mathematical problems.'

24 FEBRUARY

Chivvy

(CHIH-vee)

to tell someone repeatedly to do something (verb)

During matches, football managers have to stay in a marked-out space called the 'technical area' by the side of the pitch. They are usually seen standing right at the edge, *chivvying* their players on.

25 FEBRUARY

Bailiwick

(BAY-lih-wik)

an area in which a person is the expert or has authority (noun)

In top restaurant kitchens, the head chef is in charge but chefs de partie run their own *bailiwicks*, such as pastry, butchery or fish.

26 FEBRUARY

Glitch

(GLICH)

an unexpected and usually minor problem, often with technology (noun)

In 2012, a *glitch* in Apple's map app caused certain buildings and landmarks to seem to disappear. Many users received incorrect directions that led to impossible places, such as the middle of a lake, before the problem was fixed.

27 FEBRUARY

Impromptu

(im-PROMP-tyoo)

made or done on the spur of the moment or without preparation (adjective)

Dr Martin Luther King Jr's famous 1963 speech, 'I Have a Dream', ended up being very different from the one he had originally prepared. Dr King made the *impromptu* decision to ditch his speech and speak about his dreams for the future when gospel singer Mahalia Jackson shouted, 'Tell them about the dream, Martin!'

28 FEBRUARY

Squeamish

(SKWEE-mish)

easily nauseated or disgusted by something (adjective)

Many future doctors need to get over being *squeamish* about blood. Scientists say gradual exposure can work. For example, it helps to say the word 'blood' first, then write the word 'blood', then look at a picture of blood, and then finally see the real thing.

29 FEBRUARY

Quadrennial

(kwod-REN-ee-uhl)

occurring every four years (adjective)

The actual time it takes Earth to rotate around the Sun is 365.24 days. Most years have 365 days, but every four years we add a day on 29 February to get the calendar back in sync. 'Leap days' typically occur every four years in a *quadrennial* pattern. However, centurial years (those marking the beginning of a century, like 1700, 1800 and 1900) that aren't divisible by 400 do not get a leap day.

Story of the Month

No one could ever say my family isn't adventurous. On our last ***impromptu*** holiday, we rented a ***dilapidated*** cabin for a ***potholing*** trip in search of mushrooms. My parents are amateur ***mycophiles***, but I think they have some ***delusion*** that they're experts. Still, my mum was the ***mastermind*** of our trip and handled all obstacles with ***aplomb***. She wasn't at all ***squeamish*** about having to ***grapple*** with the slime and mud inside the caves. Mum and Dad hunted for mushrooms in ***tandem***, while I trailed behind.

I wish my parents didn't have quite so much ***wanderlust***. ***Quadrennial*** holidays would be perfect! I'm a ***bibliophile*** – and a ***logophile***. I have ***oodles*** of fun reading good books, but I'm a ***fusspot*** when it comes to the ***glitches*** that occur in the great outdoors. I'm ***incorrigible*** that way. I ***yelp*** when an insect lands on my arm and ***chivvy*** my parents to head home. I am hardly ***docile*** on these adventures.

It would be great if my parents were ***cinephiles***, and we could ***collaborate*** on plans for a relaxing night at the movies. If they were ***ailurophiles***, we could stay at home with our cats. If only they were ***turophiles***, we could eat cheese indoors and avoid exposure to the elements! But the fact remains that my parents are natural-born adventurers. In the future, I promise not to ***sabotage*** my parents' plans with my ***woebegone*** protests. Travel is their ***bailiwick*** and if they want to explore, I will always be ready for a ***punctual*** start.

Ma

rch

1 MARCH

Cahoots

(kuh-HOOTS)

a secret partnership (noun)

In 1963, a group of 15 British criminals working in *cahoots* carried out the Great Train Robbery. They escaped with £2.6 million, which was a record at the time. Most of the gang members were eventually caught, but the money was never fully recovered.

2 MARCH

Serendipitous

(SEHR-uhn-DIP-ih-tuhs)

happening by chance, with a positive result (adjective)

British actor and rapper Riz Ahmed met his wife, the novelist Fatima Faheen Mirza, through a *serendipitous* event. The pair happened to sit down at the same table in a New York café, and both reached for the same laptop port. Ahmed described their chance encounter as 'a very modern way of meeting'.

3 MARCH

Mishmash

(MISH-mash)

a confusing mixture of things (noun)

Sometimes, the whole is greater than the sum of its parts. That's the case in Bulgaria, where a *mishmash* of ingredients makes up one of the nation's most popular dishes. It includes eggs, red and green peppers, tomatoes, onions, garlic, parsley and feta cheese cooked together in an omelette that is called 'mish-mash'.

4 MARCH

Panache

(puh-NASH)

an elaborate or colourful display of style (noun)

Swedish opera star Jenny Lind was known for both her voice and for her *panache*. In the 1850s, clothing vendors used Lind's name and likeness to sell gloves, bonnets, shawls and other fashionable garments of the day.

5 MARCH

Liberate

(LIB-uh-rayt)

to set free (verb)

In 2010, entertainer Lady Gaga told an interviewer, 'I aspire to try to be a teacher to my young fans... I want to *liberate* them, I want to free them of their fears and make them feel... that they can create their own space in the world.'

6 MARCH

Hurly-burly

(HUR-lee-BUR-lee)

busy, noisy activity (noun)

Just before the Christian season of Lent begins, the city of Rio de Janeiro, Brazil, puts on what has been called 'the greatest show on Earth': the Rio Carnival. For five days the streets become a *hurly-burly* of parties, parades and samba dancing.

7 MARCH

Madcap

(MAD-kap)

very foolish, reckless or wild (adjective)

In 1921, Bessie Coleman became the first African-American woman and Native American to earn a pilot's licence. Barred from US flying schools, she travelled to Europe to do her training. On her return, she took up stunt flying and quickly became a star, entertaining crowds at air shows with *madcap* manoeuvres and daredevil dives.

8 MARCH

Avuncular

(uh-VUNK-yoo-luh)

kind or friendly like an uncle (adjective)

In the film *Mary Poppins*, Mary's uncle Albert is a jovial fellow who loves it when visitors come round. This *avuncular* man is so cheerful and friendly that he fills up with 'laughing gas' and floats into the air.

Words When You Need Them

Sometimes, you just can't think of a word for an object – or maybe you never knew it in the first place. Fortunately, there are plenty of words to use as substitutes.

9 MARCH

Doodah

(DOO-dah)

a small object whose common name is unknown or forgotten (noun)

The *doodah* that looks like a screwdriver with a sharp point at the end is called an awl. Awls are used to make holes in leather, wood and other tough material.

10 MARCH

Whatsit

(WOT-sit)

a thing or person whose name is unknown or forgotten or unmentionable (noun)

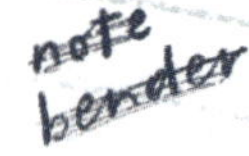

The *whatsit* on an electric guitar that rock stars use to pulse or 'bend' notes is called a vibrato arm or a whammy bar.

11 MARCH

Gizmo

~~circle~~ ~~bulb~~

(GIZ-moh)

a usually small mechanical or electronic device (noun)

A ring light is a *gizmo* that can be used when taking close-up photographs or making videos. This circle of light eliminates shadows and brings out a subject's natural skin tone.

12 MARCH

Thingamajig

~~wing~~ ~~point~~

(THING-uh-muh-jig)

something whose name you have forgotten or do not know (noun)

The upturned *thingamajig* at the end of an aeroplane wing is called a winglet. Winglets reduce the air currents that push down against the wing, increasing the plane's fuel efficiency.

13 MARCH

Banger

••••••••••

(BANG-uh)

an old car that is in poor condition (noun)

People who enjoy an adventure holiday can book themselves into a *banger* rally. First, you'll need to buy a car – but there is a limit on how much you can spend, sometimes as low as £100. With your team, you'll then drive from one country to another, passing checkpoints and camping in fields.

14 MARCH

Devour

(dih-VOWR)

to eat up hungrily (verb)

Cookie Monster is best known for scoffing cookies on *Sesame Street*, but that's not the only thing he eats. The big blue monster has been known to *devour* telephones, mailboxes, machines and anything else that crosses his hungry path.

15 MARCH

Rendezvous

(RON-day-voo)

a meeting that is planned and sometimes secret (noun)

People aren't the only ones who have *rendezvous*. Space vehicles do a set of orbital manoeuvres to have a rendezvous with each other. In some cases, the rendezvous – coming very close to one another – is followed by a docking, when the two vehicles make contact.

16 MARCH

Captivating

(KAP-tih-vay-ting)

attractive and interesting in a way that holds your attention (adjective)

The internet is full of images of cats and dogs, many of them earning huge amounts of money through advertisers. Tardar Sauce (aka Grumpy Cat) may not have been the obvious internet star with her permanently down-turned mouth, but millions of followers later, and with her own merchandising line, she proved to be every bit as *captivating* as the cute kittens.

17 MARCH

Concentric

(kon-SEN-trik)

having the same centre (adjective)

A standard archery target consists of ten evenly spaced *concentric* circles. The two centre circles are yellow, followed by two red rings, two blue rings, two black rings and two white rings. Archers score points based on where their arrows land and earn ten points when arrows hit the centre circle.

18 MARCH

Peruse

(puh-ROOZ)

to look at or read something closely and thoroughly (verb)

The Vatican Secret Archives in Rome were founded by Pope Paul V in the 1600s and are closed to the public. Historians lucky enough to *peruse* the archives have discovered interesting papers from the Roman Catholic Church's history, including a document that offers a knighthood to composer Mozart for his contributions to the Church.

Wild Weather

These weather words can make you feel the heat or send a chill down your spine.

20 MARCH

Balmy

(BAH-mee)

warm, calm and pleasant (adjective)

Countries located along Earth's equator have some of the best weather in the world. These tropical regions, including countries like Ecuador, Colombia and Indonesia, have *balmy* temperatures between 21 and 32 degrees Celsius for most of the year.

19 MARCH

Blustery

(BLUSS-tuh-ree)

blowing in strong, noisy gusts (adjective)

On 10 April 1996, scientists on Barrow Island in Australia recorded *blustery* winds with speeds of up to 407 kilometres per hour during a tropical storm.

21 MARCH

Cold snap

(KOLD SNAP)

a brief period of very cold weather (noun)

Scientists at a research station in Antarctica observed a temperature of -89 degrees Celsius during a brutal *cold snap* in 1983.

22 MARCH

Scorcher

(SKOR-chuh)

a very hot day (noun)

Residents of Death Valley in California, USA, are used to hot weather. But one *scorcher* in the summer of 2020 caused temperatures to hit a whopping 54 degrees Celsius.

23 MARCH

Cyclone

(SYE-klohn)

an extremely large, powerful and destructive storm with very high winds that turn around an area of low pressure (noun)

In 2016, Severe Tropical Cyclone Winston became the strongest ever *cyclone* to hit land in the southern hemisphere. Heavy rains and winds spiralled at nearly 300 kilometres per hour off the coast of Fiji.

24 MARCH

White-out

(WYTE-owt)

a type of snowstorm in which clouds and blowing or falling snow make it very difficult to see (noun)

In 1979, two Dutch friends on a UK road trip were caught in a *white-out* in the Yorkshire Dales that forced them to a stop. Trapped in their car overnight, they narrowly avoided freezing to death by forcing down a window the next morning and squeezing out through the gap.

25 MARCH

Swanky

(SWANK-ee)

stylish or fancy, sometimes in a showy manner (adjective)

Having pledged to give away 99 per cent of his $100-billion fortune, American businessman Warren Buffett isn't interested in a *swanky* lifestyle. He even lives in the same house he bought in the 1950s for $31,500. (It is worth over 20 times that now, and Buffet describes it as the 'third-best investment' he ever made.)

26 MARCH

Zigzag

(ZIG-zag)

to move along a path that has a series of short, sharp turns or angles (verb)

Lightning *zigzags* from the clouds as it reaches down to discharge its built-up electricity by striking the ground.

27 MARCH

Humdinger

(HUM-DING-er)

a person or thing that is striking or extraordinary (noun)

The 2021 women's final of the US Open Tennis Championships was a *humdinger* of a game. Britain's Emma Raducanu and Canada's Leylah Fernandez were the first teenagers to compete in the final since 1999. Both players performed brilliantly, with Raducanu ultimately winning the title – just months after finishing her secondary school exams.

28 MARCH

Orderly

(OR-duh-lee)

arranged in some order or pattern (adjective)

The British have a reputation for *orderly* queueing which may have originated during World War II when the government encouraged its citizens to do their duty and take their turn by waiting patiently in line to collect their rations.

29 MARCH

Earworm

(EER-werm)

a song or melody that keeps repeating in your mind (noun)

Some studies have tried to answer the question of why *earworms* get stuck in a person's head. Research shows that they are most likely to occur when a person is engaged in a routine activity, such as cleaning your room or brushing your teeth.

30 MARCH

Motley

(MOT-lee)

made up of unlike people or things (adjective)

The Wizard of Oz is a classic film musical following the adventures of a *motley* group of travelling companions. Dorothy, her dog Toto, a scarecrow, tinman and lion all seek the wizard's help and set off along the Yellow Brick Road to find him.

31 MARCH

Mojo

(MOH-joh)

a power that may seem magical and that allows someone to be very effective or successful (noun)

After some early losses in 2018, French football player Anthony Martial scored key goals that helped lead his team, Manchester United, to victory. When asked to comment on Martial's talents, British footballing legend Andy Cole said that Martial 'has got his confidence back now. He has his *mojo* back...'

Story of the Month

Last week, on a ***blustery*** day in the middle of a ***cold snap***, my cat Tatiana ***liberated*** herself from our home and went on a ***madcap*** adventure through town. It was a ***humdinger*** of a journey, which I can recap thanks to a ***mishmash*** of texts from my ***avuncular*** neighbour, who was able to spot Tatiana from his attic window despite the ***white-out*** conditions.

After taking a few ***concentric*** laps around our house, Tatiana made her way to a ***rendezvous*** with her dog friend Scout, who had dug an ***orderly*** path through the snow from our front door to the street. From there, Tatiana ***zigzagged*** across the town square, past an old ***banger***, to ***peruse*** the ***gizmos*** on display at the DIY shop. Tatiana finds that shop ***captivating***, even though she has no use for the ***doodahs***, ***whatsits*** and ***thingamajigs*** they sell there. I think the owner gives her treats that she quickly ***devours***.

Tatiana certainly does things with ***panache***. I wouldn't be surprised if she moves to the beat of a fun and lively ***earworm***. The small cat skipped around a ***motley*** crew of townspeople who were shovelling snow in the square. I worried that Tatiana might get lost in all the ***hurly-burly***. But it was ***serendipitous*** that just as she was getting tired, our neighbour passed by on his ***swanky*** snowplough and gave her a lift home.

As an escape artist, Tatiana certainly hasn't lost her ***mojo***. And when she's in ***cahoots*** with Scout, there's no stopping her. I just hope the next time she decides to visit her friend, she chooses a ***balmy*** summer day or even a ***scorcher***. If that cat escapes during another weather emergency, like a ***cyclone***, she can find her own way home!

ril

1 APRIL

Turbulent

(TER-byoo-luhnt)

causing or being in a state of unrest, violence or disturbance (adjective)

Even very large boats get tossed around by ocean waves. Wind patterns, water temperatures and underwater earthquakes can all cause *turbulent* seas.

2 APRIL

Escalate

(ESS-kuh-layt)

to increase in extent, volume, number, amount, intensity or scope (verb)

In 1900, the Otis Elevator Company built a new moving stairway that they called an 'escalator' for an international exhibition in Paris, where it won the Grand Prize. Demand for the escalator instantly *escalated* and mechanical stairways popped up around the world.

3 APRIL

Sputter

(SPUT-uh)

to make explosive popping sounds (verb)

People aren't the only ones who *sputter*. When an engine sputters, it's not a good sign. It could mean that it is about to run out of fuel or that parts in the fuel or exhaust system are dirty or worn out.

4 APRIL

Egad

(ih-GAD)

used as a mild oath or an exclamation of surprise (interjection)

A word like *egad* is often called a ‘minced oath’ – a more appropriate version of another expression that is considered unacceptable. In cultures where it’s considered sinful to say the Lord’s name in vain, egad is a stand-in for ‘oh God’. Other minced oaths include ‘gosh’ and ‘heck’.

5 APRIL

Brouhaha

(BROO-hah-hah)

great excitement or concern about something (noun)

In 2000, a bomb-sniffing German shepherd doing a sweep of a New York museum caused quite a *brouhaha* when it detected gunpowder. The dog led its handlers to an empty 30-centimetre-long artillery shell used in the American Civil War. It could smell the remains of 135-year-old gunpowder!

6 APRIL

Grotesque

(groh-TESK)

ugly or distorted in a repulsive or comical way (adjective)

Most mirrors are flat so that when you stand in front of them they reflect a true image. Funhouse mirrors have curved surfaces so that they distort the reflection. Concave mirrors curve outwards, squashing the image, while convex mirrors elongate the image by curving inwards. Used together they can produce some rather *grotesque* reflections.

7 APRIL

Colossal

(kuh-LOSS-uhl)

extremely large or great (adjective)

The largest known animal to exist on planet Earth is the blue whale. This *colossal* mammal is bigger than any dinosaur ever discovered and can grow to be over 149,685 kilograms – about the size of 30 elephants!

8 APRIL

Aghast

(uh-GAHST)

struck with terror, surprise or horror (adjective)

In his 1842 poem 'The Wreck of the Hesperus', Henry Wadsworth Longfellow writes about a maiden caught in an ocean storm and the fisherman who discovers her. Longfellow writes,

> At daybreak, on the bleak sea-beach,
> A fisherman stood *aghast*,
> To see the form of a maiden fair,
> Lashed close to a drifting mast.

9 APRIL

Flummox

(FLUM-uhks)

to confuse (verb)

It took Ernő Rubik, inventor of the Rubik's Cube, a whole month to solve his own puzzle. With six sides, each with nine blocks of colour, there are apparently 43 quintillion possible combinations – it's no surprise people are *flummoxed* by it. But not everyone. The record for the fastest solving of the cube is held by Yusheng Du at 3.47 seconds.

10 APRIL

Trickle

(TRIK-uhl)

a thin, slow stream of water, people or things (noun)

Italian astronaut Luca Parmitano was taking a spacewalk in 2013 when he felt a *trickle* of cold water on his head. Before long, his helmet was filling with water. 'I experienced what it's like to be a goldfish in a fishbowl', he said after safely returning to his spacecraft. He later learned the water had leaked from his spacesuit's cooling system.

Baby Animals

Come and meet these cute little infant words before they grow up.

11 APRIL

Fawn

(FAWN)

a young deer (noun)

Fawns are born with white spots on their back to help them blend in with their surroundings. The spots fade after a few months.

12 APRIL

Cygnet

(SIG-nuht)

a young swan (noun)

Although *cygnets* can run and swim a few hours after hatching, they stay with their parents for several months. Cygnets become adults after three or four years.

13 APRIL

Elver

(EL-vuh)

a young eel (noun)

Eel eggs hatch into larvae, then become glass eels, then *elvers*. Elvers are about 10 centimetres long. As adults, some eels can grow up to 3.3 metres long.

14 APRIL

Peachick

(PEE-chik)

the chick of any of three species of large birds called peafowl (noun)

Adult female peafowl are called peahens and adult males are called peacocks. Peacocks display long, multicoloured feathers, while peahens have shorter feathers. The *peachicks* have all of their feathers when they hatch.

15 APRIL

Spat

(SPAT)

a young oyster, clam, mussel or other mollusc with a shell that has two parts connected by a hinge (noun)

Oyster *spats* attach themselves to a resting spot, where they stay as they grow into adult oysters. That process can take two to three years.

16 APRIL

Puffling

(PUFF-ling)

a young puffin (noun)

Puffins dig burrows to lay their egg in and look after their *puffling* once it's hatched. The adults abandon the puffling just before it's ready to leave the nest and head out to sea.

17 APRIL

Nevertheless

(NEV-uh-thuh-LESS)

even so; however (adverb)

The reign of Queen Elizabeth I is viewed by historians as a golden age. Under her leadership, England warded off an invasion by the Spanish Armada. Elizabeth said, 'Though the sex to which I belong is considered weak, you will *nevertheless* find me a rock that bends to no wind.'

18 APRIL

Affable

(AF-uh-bul)

friendly and sociable (adjective)

Beware the *affable* fox, the folk tales warn us. From the gingerbread man who hitches a fatal ride on the back of a friendly fox, to Aesop's crow, tricked into dropping its cheese by a sweet-talking fox, to Henny Penny, who gets invited into Foxy Loxy's house for tea without realising she is to be the main course – the message is clear: foxes cannot be trusted.

19 APRIL

Salinity

•••••••••••

(suh-LIN-ih-tee)

the amount of dissolved salts in water or another liquid (noun)

The concentration of salts in a body of water, or *salinity*, is measured in parts per million (ppm). Fresh water contains less than 1,000 ppm. Seawater contains a high salinity of about 35,000 ppm, which gives the water its salty taste and smell.

20 APRIL

Kibosh

(KYE-bosh)

something that serves as a check or stop – usually used in the phrase *put the kibosh on* (noun)

In April 2010 an Icelandic volcano erupted, sending up huge plumes of ash that caused airports to close across Europe. Not only did this put the *kibosh* on people's holidays, it meant the Barcelona football team had to travel about 1,000 kilometres by bus to get to their UEFA Champions League semi-final in Milan.

21 APRIL

Indubitable

(in-DYOO-bih-tuh-bul)

beyond question or doubt (adjective)

The following facts are *indubitable*:

- There are 11 letters in the word indubitable.
- 21 April falls on page 110.
- The 21st follows the 20th.

22 APRIL

Jolt

• • • • •

(JOLT)

a sudden feeling of shock, surprise or disappointment (noun)

Electric eels aren't actually eels at all. They are closely related to catfish. It is thought that the ancient Egyptians caught small electric catfish and used them to give shocks to arthritis sufferers as treatment. A *jolt* from a large Amazonian electric eel would be much more powerful. Early explorers reported horses being stunned and knocked off their feet by them.

23 APRIL

Roundabout

(ROWN-duh-bowt)

not following a short direct route (adjective); a junction where traffic must travel in one direction around a circular area (noun)

The shortest distance between two places is not always the quickest way to get from one to the other. *Roundabout* routes that use faster roads and avoid traffic light junctions can keep drivers moving even at very busy times.

24 APRIL

Waver

(WAY-vuh)

to go back and forth between choices or opinions; to be uncertain about what you think (verb)

British singer-songwriter FKA twigs described her experience in the music industry, saying, 'Sometimes I feel 15; other times I feel fully grown and mature and handling all my business. It can *waver* from day to day, hour to hour.'

Words for Nothing

The English language makes much ado about nothing. Here are four examples:

25 APRIL

Nil

(NIL)

nothing; zero (noun)

Before having an operation, patients might be given the instruction '*nil* by mouth', which means they shouldn't eat or drink anything in the run up to surgery. Nil is a contraction of the Latin word for nothing, *nihil*.

26 APRIL

Naught

(NAWT)

nothing (pronoun)

Boardmasters Festival is an annual event in Cornwall that combines live music with surfing and skateboarding competitions. In 2019, festival organisers learned that all their planning was for *naught* when bad weather forced them to cancel the event hours before opening day.

27 APRIL

Diddly-squat

(DID-uh-lee-skwot)

the least amount; nothing at all (noun)

Winning the lottery can be a dream come true, but don't lose your lottery ticket! In 2001, Martyn and Kay Tott won £3 million in the UK lottery. Unfortunately, they lost their ticket and ended up receiving *diddly-squat*.

28 APRIL

Zilch

(ZILCH)

zero; nothing (noun)

In 2018, two McDonald's customers sued the fast-food company for $5 million for charging the same price for a Quarter Pounder burger with or without cheese. The customers thought a Quarter Pounder without cheese should be less expensive. A judge disagreed and dismissed the case, leaving both customers with *zilch*.

29 APRIL

Dilly-dally

(DIL-ee-dal-ee)

to move or act too slowly; to waste time (verb)

Perhaps it's not surprising that there have been at least four racehorses named Don't Dilly Dally. The one who best lived up to the name was a mare from New Zealand who definitely did not *dilly-dally*. She won four times, came in second twice and came in third six times.

30 APRIL

Swagger

(SWAG-uh)

a way of walking or behaving that shows bold or brash self-confidence (noun)

In 2008, a British man was charged with burglary after medical experts identified him on CCTV by his walk. The man had a distinctive bow-legged *swagger* like that of legendary cowboy actor John Wayne. He was jailed for two years.

Story of the Month

There's no ***roundabout*** way to say this. When I got home from my visit to the aquarium today, I found an ***elver*** in my pocket. I put my hand in there and with a ***jolt***, I felt the slimy thing squirming around. I was ***aghast***, as well as ***flummoxed***. I had seen lots of baby animals: ***pufflings***, ***cygnets***, ***spats***, ***peachicks*** and even a ***fawn***. But I didn't remember any elvers!

Now I know ***diddly-squat*** about eels and their offspring – ***zilch***. ***Egad***, what if I killed the little thing? I went online and learned that most elvers live in salty water, so I got out our big saucepan. I started with a ***trickle*** of water, then more, and added salt, hoping I had the right ***salinity***. I was relieved when he started to swim around. When my mum came home, you can imagine her expression: it was ***grotesque***. Before the situation could ***escalate*** into a ***brouhaha***, I ***sputtered*** out what had happened.

After that ***turbulent*** moment, my mum, in her ***indubitable*** wisdom, put the ***kibosh*** on my worries and told me to call the aquarium. I ***wavered*** a bit because I thought I might get into a ***colossal*** amount of trouble. I was nervous that all my apologies would be for ***naught***, and I would have virtually ***nil*** to show for my efforts. ***Nevertheless***, my explanation satisfied the ***affable*** general manager. She said I should bring back the elver without ***dilly-dallying***. And I did, with a bit of ***swagger***. After all, I had managed to keep the little fellow alive!

ay
....

1 MAY

Flibbertigibbet

(FLIB-uh-tee-JIB-ut)

a silly flighty person (noun)

During World War II, an American spy named Gertrude Legendre was captured in France by the Nazis. She survived six months of interrogation by behaving like a *flibbertigibbet* and hiding her true identity. Eventually she escaped to Switzerland.

2 MAY

Antenna

(an-TEN-uh)

a metallic device (such as a rod, wire or dish) used to transmit or receive radio waves (noun)

The National Aeronautics and Space Administration (NASA) in the United States has a 'Deep Space Network' that detects tiny radio signals from space. In order to receive these faraway waves, they use dish *antennas* over 70 metres wide. That's wider than an Olympic-sized football pitch!

Oh my! I didn't think I would win. I really don't know what to say. I don't have a speech prepared. I want to thank all the other nominees. You were terrific. I want to thank everyone who helped me get to where I am today. When I was little, I always dreamed I would win an award like this. And I want to tell everyone that dreams do come true. All you have to do is believe. I'd like to thank my parents for their love and support. I'd also like to thank my assistant, my hairdresser, my lawyer, my personal trainer, my dietician, my teachers, my doctors, my friends, my cousins, my grandparents, my godparents, my agent, my manager...

3 MAY

Wordy

(WER-dee)

containing more words than necessary (adjective)

In the 1940s, Oscar winners uttered an average of 113 words in their Academy Award acceptance speeches. Today, winners give *wordy* speeches that typically exceed 250 words.

4 MAY

Verisimilitude

(vair-ih-sih-MILL-uh-tyood)

the quality of seeming real (noun)

Novelist Jane Austen is often considered a master of *verisimilitude* because she created characters that feel like actual people to her readers. To this day, historians continue searching for real people who may have inspired Austen's characters, because they seem too real to be fictional.

5 MAY

Gargoyle

(GAHR-goyl)

a strange or ugly human or animal figure that sticks out from the roof of a building (such as a church) (noun)

Gargoyles aren't just decorative. The Old French word '*gargouille*', meaning throat, offers a clue to their purpose, which was to protect the walls of a building by spouting rainwater safely away through their mouths. Used widely on churches in the Middle Ages, their scary faces were supposed to remind people of the threat of evil, and the protection offered by the Church.

6 MAY

Axle

• • • • • • •

(AK-suhl)

the rod or shaft a wheel rests on as it spins (noun)

Engineer George Washington Gale Ferris Jr created the first Ferris Wheel in 1893. Two 42-metre steel towers supported the giant wheel, which was connected by a 13-metre *axle*. At the time, the axle was the largest piece of forged steel ever made.

7 MAY

Raconteur

(rak-on-TER)

someone who is good at telling stories (noun)

American poet Amanda Gorman is known as the gifted *raconteur* who recited her poem 'The Hill We Climb' at the 2021 US presidential inauguration. Amanda later revealed that she'd previously struggled with a speech impediment. To overcome it, she rapped along with the musical *Hamilton* to improve her diction.

8 MAY

Retronym

(RET-roh-nim)

a new term used to distinguish the older version of something from the more recent version (noun)

The first bicycles had very large front wheels with small back wheels. In the late 19th century, 'safety bicycles' with equal-sized wheels were invented. Eventually, the first bicycles were given the *retronym* 'ordinary bicycles' to tell them apart from the newer, safer bikes.

Digging up the Past

To learn about the past, archaeologists go digging for some of these words.

9 MAY

Fossil

• • • • • • •

(FOSS-uhl)

a remnant (such as a bone) or trace (such as a footprint) of a living thing from the distant past that is preserved in rock (noun)

In 2010, scientists discovered the *fossil* of a giant penguin in Peru that lived nearly 36 million years ago. The penguin, which was given the nickname 'Pedro', had brown and grey feathers and was nearly twice as heavy as the emperor penguin, the largest species of penguin known today.

10 MAY

Relic

• • • • • •

(REL-ik)

an object surviving from an earlier time (noun)

In May 2013, ancient mollusc shells were discovered at a construction site in Yuyao, China. These shells are *relics* from early humans who lived in Eastern China approximately 8,000 years ago and ate these oyster-like sea creatures.

11 MAY

Stratum

• • • • • • • • • • •

(STRAH-tuhm)

a layer of rock or soil (noun) (plural *strata*)

Over time, changes in the environment create new layers of soil on the ground. As these layers build up, the weight of the top ones turns the lower ones to stone. A *stratum* of hardened ash may be the remains of a volcanic explosion that happened millions of years ago.

12 MAY

Artefact

(AHR-tih-fakt)

an object made by people in the past (noun)

Artefacts discovered in the waters of Lake Titicaca in Bolivia revealed details about the Tiwanaku Empire which lasted from 600 to 1000 CE. Gold medallions, stone carvings and religious figures dredged from the bottom suggest that the Tiwanaku people made religious pilgrimages to the lake.

13 MAY

Excavate

(EK-skuh-vayt)

to uncover (something) by digging away and removing the earth that covers it (verb)

In 2013, a team of archaeologists began to *excavate* fossils in the Rising Star Cave system in South Africa. They have since discovered over 1,550 skeletal fragments from ancient human ancestors.

14 MAY

Coprolite

(KO-pruh-lyte)

a piece of fossilised dung (noun)

Grass particles discovered in dinosaur *coprolites* near India proved that some dinosaurs ate grass, and that these plants were evolving at around the same time as dinosaurs.

15 MAY

Beneficiary

(ben-uh-FISH-uh-ree)

a person, group or organisation that receives money or property when someone dies (noun)

When billionaire Leona Helmsley died in 2007, she left some of her fortune to her nine-year-old dog, Trouble. The small Maltese became the *beneficiary* of $12 million and was hidden from the public to keep her safe from potential robbers.

16 MAY

Uncouth

(un-KOOTH)

behaving in a rude way; not polite or socially acceptable (adjective)

When Goldilocks breaks into a house, helps herself to the food, destroys the furniture and goes to sleep in one of the beds, it's no surprise that the homeowners take offence. This famous fairy tale has many versions. In one of the earliest to be written down, the central character is an old woman who is punished for such *uncouth* behaviour by being thrown on to the steeple of St Paul's Cathedral!

17 MAY

Procrastinator

(pruh-KRASS-tuh-nay-tuh)

a person who frequently puts off doing things (noun)

Surprisingly, famed artist and inventor Leonardo da Vinci was a *procrastinator*. When asked to complete a project for a church in Milan, Italy, da Vinci said he could have it done in six months. The project took twenty-five years to complete.

18 MAY

Incognito

(in-kog-NEE-toh)

with your true identity kept secret, often using a different name or a disguise (adverb)

British actor Daniel Radcliffe once wore a Spider-Man suit in order to walk around the international comic book convention, Comic-Con, *incognito*. He adopted an American accent and even took photographs with people who were unaware that it was the movie star in disguise.

19 MAY

Jubilee

(joo-bih-LEE)

a celebration at the time of a special anniversary (noun)

A golden *jubilee* refers to a 50th anniversary. To celebrate Emperor Showa's golden jubilee as the ruler of Japan, he had a park created to commemorate the occasion. Showa Memorial Park in Tokyo spans nearly 400 acres and features lush lawns, walking trails, fountains and ponds.

20 MAY

Fuddy-duddy

(FUD-ee-dud-ee)

a person with old-fashioned ideas and attitudes (noun)

At age 96, American fashion icon Iris Apfel became the oldest person to have a Barbie doll made after her. 'I never want to be an old *fuddy-duddy*', Apfel said. 'I hold the self-proclaimed record for being the World's Oldest Living Teenager.'

21 MAY

Sangfroid

(song-FRWAH)

the ability to stay cool and composed in difficult or dangerous situations (noun)

In 1982, Josephine Reynolds became the first female firefighter in the United Kingdom. She displayed incredible *sangfroid* while fighting forest fires and responding to emergency traffic accidents, which helped open the door for other women to join the fire service.

22 MAY

Alias

(AY-lee-uhss)

an additional name that someone sometimes uses instead of their given name (noun)

In the DC Comics universe, Superman is an *alias* for the journalist Clark Kent. In several iconic stories, Clark darts into a phone box to secretly transform into Superman to save the day.

Shipwreck

Strap on your life jacket and get ready to take a dive in! When ships sink, these words float to the top.

23 MAY

Castaway

(KAHST-uh-way)

a person who has been left alone in an isolated place as a result of a storm, shipwreck, etc. (noun)

In 1858 a ship, the *Saint-Paul*, hit a reef off the coast of New Guinea and was wrecked. A cabin boy named Narcisse Pelletier and some others survived, travelling by longboat for more than 1,000 kilometres to Australia, where Narcisse was abandoned and became a *castaway*. He was eventually rescued by local Aboriginal people and lived with them for the next 17 years before being spotted by a British ship captain and taken back to France.

24 MAY

Jetsam

(JET-suhm)

objects that are thrown overboard from a ship to lighten the ship's load (noun)

In 1782, a British ship destined for the United States got stuck in a sandbar off the coast of Florida. While all the passengers made it off safely, historians believe that the crew tossed a heavy lead pump, cannons and other *jetsam* overboard in an attempt to lighten the ship's load and free it from the sand.

25 MAY

Salvage

(SAL-vij)

to rescue or save from wreckage or ruin (verb)

In the 1780s, the British ship *Hartwell* sank along the coast of Cape Verde in Western Africa. In the 1990s, a South African company sent researchers to the bottom of the sea to *salvage* silver coins and other artefacts from the wreck.

26 MAY

Flotsam

(FLOT-suhm)

floating wreckage of a ship or its cargo (noun)

In 1997, nearly five million Lego bricks fell into the sea during a shipping voyage. This colourful *flotsam* travelled on ocean currents all around the world, with Lego bricks washing up on beaches from Europe to Australia.

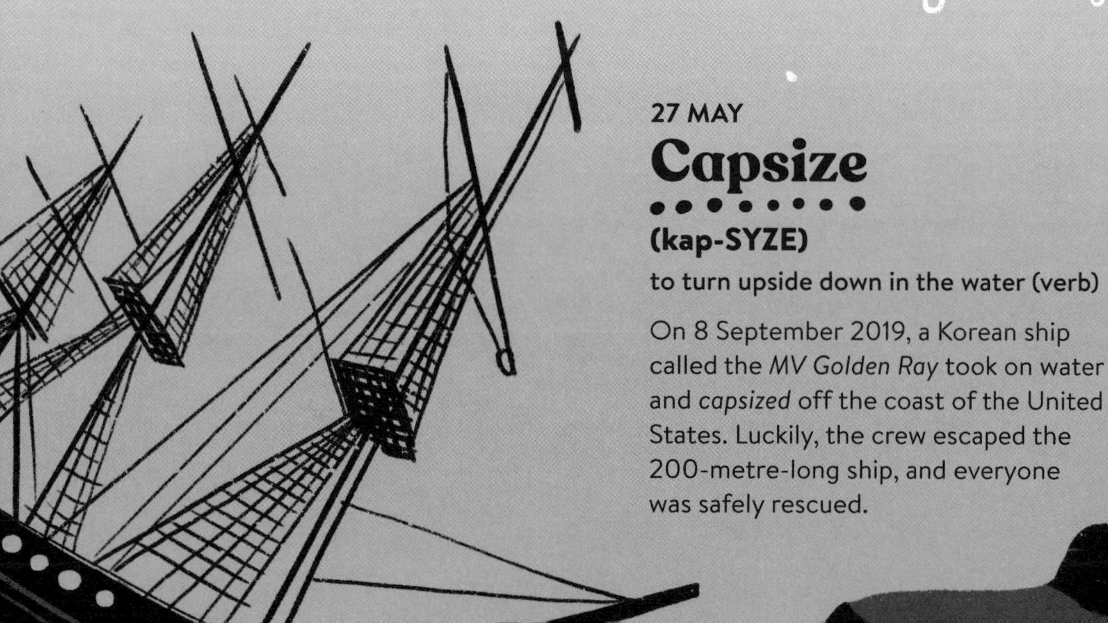

27 MAY

Capsize

(kap-SYZE)

to turn upside down in the water (verb)

On 8 September 2019, a Korean ship called the *MV Golden Ray* took on water and *capsized* off the coast of the United States. Luckily, the crew escaped the 200-metre-long ship, and everyone was safely rescued.

28 MAY

Contend

(kon-TEND)

to struggle to overcome something (verb)

'Stagecoach Mary' was the nickname given to Mary Fields, the first African American woman to become a Star Route Carrier for the US Post Office in 1895. She delivered mail in a horse-drawn stagecoach and had to *contend* with dangers like wolves, brutal weather conditions and even robbers. Despite these dangers, she never missed a day of work in eight years.

29 MAY

Skyrocket

(SKYE-roh-kit)

to rise in number quickly or suddenly (verb)

The Indian film industry is the biggest in the world, with as many as 1,800 films in different languages produced each year. Hindi-language Bollywood films, known for their big musical productions, glamourous stars and dramatic storylines, have gained a huge global following. In 2017, box office collections for Indian films outside of India *skyrocketed* to £265 million, almost triple that of the previous year.

30 MAY

Scoundrel

(SKOWN-druhl)

a person who is cruel or dishonest (noun)

Charles Ponzi was an Italian American conman who posed as a financial advisor in 1920 and promised people large sums of money on investments. The only issue though was that there were no real investments. Ponzi was simply moving money from new investors to pay off old investors, while taking money from everyone in the process. By the time he was caught, the *scoundrel* had stolen $15 million.

31 MAY

Defenestrate

(dee-FEN-uh-strayt)

to throw a person or thing out of a window (verb)

Some rock stars are notorious for their bad behaviour. In the 1970s, stories abounded of hotel rooms being trashed during parties held by rock bands on tour. In one of these, Rolling Stones guitarist Keith Richards famously *defenestrated* a TV while staying at the Andaz West Hollywood in 1972.

Story of the Month

Every Friday night, Maya and her friends play the adventure-fantasy role-playing game *The Realm of Imperium*. This week's game is a ***jubilee*** because the group has been playing for one year. Maya and her friends love going ***incognito*** as their game ***aliases***. Kamal plays a ***scoundrel*** wizard only out for himself. Daniel plays an ***uncouth*** troll with a chip on his shoulder. Noah dives into the role of a ***gargoyle*** capable of flight and strength. Rosa becomes an archer with great aim and an abundance of ***sangfroid***. And Isla becomes a ***fuddy-duddy*** robot who only plays classical music and controls sound through her ***antenna***.

Maya plays the role of the game-master. At school, Maya gets anxious and sometimes feels like a ***wordy flibbertigibbet***. But when she leads the game, she becomes a gifted ***raconteur*** capable of a ***verisimilitude*** that brings the game to life.

'This week,' she says, 'the realm must ***contend*** with evil forces while returning stolen ***relics*** and ***artefacts*** to their rightful tomb overseas.' Kamal starts the game by trading a magic potion to become a sea captain's ***beneficiary***, gaining access to the captain's ship. The players climb aboard to start their epic voyage. It doesn't take long before the mishaps begin to ***skyrocket***, until at last, disaster strikes. 'Oh no!' Maya shouts. 'A sea dragon hit the ship! We're going down!' The players desperately start throwing ***jetsam*** overboard, until the ship ***capsizes*** and they must ***defenestrate*** themselves through the portholes. Kamal, Daniel, Noah and Isla cling to ***flotsam*** in the water while Rosa dives to the sea floor to ***salvage*** the relics and artefacts. The ***castaways*** then swim to a nearby island to continue their mission.

When they reach land, Noah – who is usually a ***procrastinator*** – is the first to discover the tomb. The players turn a wheel that turns an ***axle*** to open the tomb's door. Once inside, Daniel ***excavates strata*** and removes ***fossils*** and ***coprolites*** from the dirt until he uncovers a golden box. Finally, the players place the relics and artefacts in the box to win the game. 'Nice one, everyone!' Maya tells her friends. 'Next week, we can try out the latest expansion pack called *The Realm of New Imperium*. The game we've been playing now goes by the ***retronym*** *The Realm of Old Imperium*. See you again next Friday!'

Ju

ne

1 JUNE

Befuddle

●●●●●●●●●●●●

(bih-FUD-uhl)

to confuse (verb) – often used as befuddled (adjective)

When asked about his research in a 2007 interview, astrophysicist Neil deGrasse Tyson said, ‘If a scientist is not *befuddled* by what they’re looking at, then they’re not a research scientist.’

2 JUNE

Impetus

(IM-puh-tuhss)

a force that causes something (such as a process or activity) to be done (noun)

Ever want to write an invisible message? Squeeze lemon juice into a glass, add a few drops of water and mix it together. Then, dip a paintbrush into the mixture and write a message on some paper. After it dries, heat the paper with a hair dryer and the message will reappear! Lemon juice contains acid that only darkens when heated, so the hot air acts as the *impetus* for your secret message to be revealed.

3 JUNE

Kerfuffle

(kuh-FUFF-uhl)

a disturbance or commotion typically caused by a dispute or conflict (noun)

A *kerfuffle* at a football match in 1998 has gone down in the sport's history because those involved were dressed up as giant furry animals. When the Wolverhampton Wanderers' wolf mascot found himself surrounded on the pitch at half time by Bristol City's three little pigs, he felt threatened and lashed out with a paw. The scrap that ensued was swiftly broken up by the match stewards.

4 JUNE

Bamboozle

(bam-BOO-zul)

to trick or confuse (verb)

Anansi the Spider is a character from West African folklore known to *bamboozle* people to get what he wants. In one story, Anansi tricks the Sky God, Nyame, into selling him all the stories in the universe.

5 JUNE

Domesticate

(duh-MESS-tih-kayt)

to breed or train an animal to need and accept the care of human beings (verb)

Thousands of years ago, wild chickens weighed about 900 grams and laid a small number of eggs. Humans *domesticated* the animal over time and bred it to be larger to provide more meat. Now, domestic chickens typically weigh up to 3 kilograms and often produce 200 or more eggs a year.

6 JUNE

Exasperate

(eg-ZAHS-puh-rayt)

to make (someone) very angry or annoyed (verb)

In 2014, psychologists studied why 'rage quitting' is common among video game players. They found that playing poorly and being beaten by another player, or even a computer, *exasperates* them. This threatens their ego and causes an outburst.

7 JUNE

Ruse

• • • • • • •

(ROOZ)

an action intended to deceive or trick someone (noun)

One of Aesop's fables tells the story of a wolf who wears sheepskin as a *ruse* to blend in with the flock and eat the sheep at nightfall. A hungry shepherd ruins the wolf's plan when he goes to kill a sheep for dinner... and chooses the wolf!

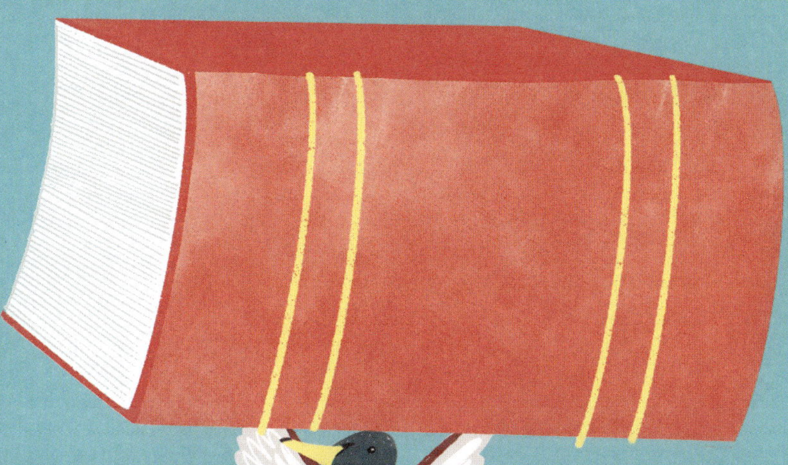

8 JUNE

Omnibus

(OM-nih-buss)

a book containing reprints of a number of works (as of a single author or on a single subject) (noun)

Writer J. R. R. Tolkien's famous novel *The Lord of the Rings* is comprised of three books: *The Fellowship of the Ring*, *The Two Towers* and *The Return of the King*. The novel is sold as an *omnibus* containing all three books plus six appendices, bringing the total word count to around half a million!

9 JUNE

Pachyderm

(PAK-ih-derm)

a type of animal that has hooves and thick skin (noun)

The rhinoceros is a type of *pachyderm*, and so are hippos and elephants. There are five different species of rhino – two found in Africa (black and white rhinos) and three in Asia (Indian, Sumatran and Javan rhinos). Rhinos love mud and are often seen rolling around in it to give them a 'mud coat' which helps keep them cool and stops insects from biting.

10 JUNE

Septillion

(sep-TIL-yuhn)

a number equal to 1 followed by 24 zeros (1,000,000,000,000,000,000,000,000) (noun)

Each year during winter, the Earth receives a *septillion* snowflakes. That's a trillion trillion!

11 JUNE

Rubberneck

(RUB-uh-nek)

to look around or stare with great curiosity; to slow down while you are driving in order to stare at something (verb)

In 2017, the company SpaceX launched a rocket in order to send satellites into space. The launch was a success, but all the people *rubbernecking* on the motorway below caused a multiple-car crash.

12 JUNE

Doppelgänger

(DOP-uhl-gang-uh)

a ghostly counterpart or lookalike of a living person (noun)

Edgar Allen Poe's horror tale *William Wilson* tells the story of a boy who meets his *doppelgänger*. Throughout William's life, his double works tirelessly to ruin his plans until William finally kills him. However, it turns out that the double was only in William's head, and he accidentally ends his own life.

Robotic Words

Check out these mechanical words and get ready for the robot revolution!

13 JUNE

Cyborg

(SYE-borg)

a creature that is part human and part machine or a person whose body contains mechanical or electrical devices that provide more power than the average human (noun)

Spanish-born artist Neil Harbisson was diagnosed with complete colour blindness as a child. Working with computer scientists, he had a sensor and antenna implanted into his brain that translates colours into sound waves. Now, Harbisson can detect ultraviolet and infrared colours invisible to the human eye in addition to colours other humans can see. Harbisson is the first *cyborg* legally recognised by a government.

14 JUNE

Android

(AN-droyd)

a robot with a human appearance (noun)

Sophia the Robot, an *android* created by scientists at Hanson Robotics in Hong Kong, captured the world's attention when she debuted in 2016. Sophia looks and talks like a human and can even recognise people's facial expressions and tone of voice.

15 JUNE

Debug

(dee-BUG)

to identify and remove errors from computer hardware or software (verb)

In February 2013, scientists lost communication with the Mars rover, *Curiosity*, due to a mechanical issue. Team members *debugged* the rover from over 200 million kilometres away and were able to recover communication three weeks later.

16 JUNE

Automation

(aw-tuh-MAY-shuhn)

the process of replacing human labour with a system of mechanical or electronic operations (noun)

As robotics improve, more jobs are being replaced by machines. The accounting firm PricewaterhouseCoopers (PwC) predicts that by 2030, nearly 30 per cent of all jobs in the UK may be eliminated due to *automation*.

17 JUNE

Actuator

(AK-tyoo-ay-ter)

the part of a machine that makes something move or operate (noun)

When you walk into a supermarket and the doors automatically open, an *actuator* is providing the energy to make the doors move.

18 JUNE

Prototype

(PROH-tuh-type)

original or first model of something from which other forms are copied or developed (noun)

In 2015, Google unveiled the *prototype* for a self-driving car. Unfortunately, the car was involved in 11 minor traffic accidents and further testing was needed.

19 JUNE

Busker

(BUSS-kuh)

someone who plays music in the street for donations (noun)

Tracy Chapman is an American singer-songwriter who rose to fame in the 1980s. Her first public performance was as a *busker* when she was at university – she wanted to make enough money to buy a Chinese take-away. She continued after that, until an impressed friend introduced her to his father, who ran a record label. 'Fast Car', one of the songs on her debut album, became a top ten hit on both sides of the Atlantic.

20 JUNE

Abhor

(uhb-HOR)

to dislike someone or something very much (verb)

Coriander is a herb similar to basil or parsley that is often used in cooking. But some people *abhor* it. That's because they have a gene that makes this popular herb taste like soap!

21 JUNE

Recumbent

(rih-KUM-buhnt)

lying down (adjective)

In the 1930s, French bicycle builder Charles Mochet shocked the world with a new kind of bike when its rider travelled at more than 45 kilometres per hour and set a new world record. Low to the ground, the design of his bike had riders in a *recumbent* position, almost lying on their backs rather than sitting upright. It caused such outrage that the International Cyclist's Union came out with a new definition of a racing bicycle that essentially banned recumbent bikes.

22 JUNE

Ecosystem

(EE-koh-siss-tuhm)

an interconnected community of living things that interact with one another and their environment (noun)

The Amazon Rainforest in South America is perhaps the world's most diverse *ecosystem*. Currently, about 390 billion trees and 10 per cent of all animal species on Earth call the Amazon Rainforest home.

23 JUNE

Squeegee

(SKWEE-jee)

a tool made out of a blade of rubber attached to a handle that is used for spreading or wiping liquid on, across or off a surface (noun)

Each year, the International Window Cleaning Association hosts a convention with an official speed-cleaning contest. Each contestant uses a *squeegee* to wipe windows clean until there are no visible streaks or smears. Judged by an expert referee, each smear detected gets a half-second penalty.

24 JUNE

Harbinger

(HAHR-bin-juh)

a person or thing that announces the arrival of another person or thing (noun)

There is a belief in the British Isles and parts of Europe that chimney sweeps are *harbingers* of good luck. Newlywed couples often hire chimney sweeps to greet them on their wedding day to ensure good luck for the future.

25 JUNE

Curlicue

(KER-lee-kyoo)

a decoratively curved line or shape (noun)

In cartoons, pigs are usually portrayed as plump pink animals with corkscrew-shaped tails. But not all species of pig have *curlicues* on their rear ends. Most wild pigs actually have straight tails.

26 JUNE

Ponder

•••••••••••

(PON-duh)

to think about or consider (something) carefully (verb)

'What is the meaning of life?' is a question that has been *pondered* by philosophers, theologians, scientists and probably everyone who has ever lived. In Douglas Adams's series of comic science-fiction books, *The Hitchhiker's Guide to the Galaxy*, a supercomputer called Deep Thought ponders this question for 7.5 million years, and finally comes up with the answer '42'.

27 JUNE

Turbine

(TUR-byne)

a spinning engine that turns the movement of water, steam, gas, air or another fluid into energy (noun)

Windmills located in the town of Nashtifan, Iran, are some of the oldest in the world. Made from clay, straw and wood, the *turbines* can withstand winds of up to 120 kilometres per hour.

28 JUNE

Demolish

(dih-MOL-ish)

to destroy, tear down or take apart (verb)

There are several ways to *demolish* a building. One of the most common is with a wrecking ball that is repeatedly swung into or dropped on the building. The most spectacular method, though, is by implosion, where the building is blown up in such a way that it safely collapses in on itself. By carefully planning where to place the explosives and when to set them off, even really tall buildings can be demolished without affecting others nearby.

29 JUNE

Honorary

(ON-uh-rair-ee)

given or elected in recognition of achievement or service without the usual requirements (adjective)

In 1981, a black dog named Bosco beat two people in an election and was named *honorary* mayor of Sunol, California, USA. Though the current mayor is a human, a bronze statue of the friendly dog now stands permanently at the town's post office.

30 JUNE

Pompadour

(POM-puh-dor)

a style of hairdressing in which the hair is combed into a high mound in front (noun)

In Japan, members of the modern-day subculture group, the Tokyo Rockabilly Club, sport gravity-defying *pompadours* and dance in Yoyogi Park to celebrate the era of 1950s American rock 'n' roll.

Story of the Month

Lucy always wanted to be a comic book writer. The ***impetus*** for this career path was the old ***omnibus*** sci-fi comic book, Orion Colt: ***Cyborg*** Superstar, which she read as a kid. The series follows space-travelling robot Orion Colt, a ***busker*** turned folk-singing sensation with a ***curlicue pompadour*** and a state-of-the-art ***prototype*** laser guitar. His sidekick is QE-5, an ***exasperated android*** with a built-in ***squeegee***. The robots battle Overlord Dorn, an evil force who emits a foul smell as a ***harbinger*** of impending doom. Dorn seeks to destroy the ***ecosystem*** of every planet so he can control more than a ***septillion*** living organisms for himself.

In Lucy's favourite adventure, Orion holds a concert and gets Overlord Dorn to attend. Riding atop a ***domesticated pachyderm***, Dorn moves through the ***rubbernecking*** crowd to get closer to Orion. But when he reaches the stage, Dorn realises that the singer is not Orion, but his ***doppelgänger***! The concert was merely a ***ruse*** for Orion to sneak on to Dorn's ship. As Dorn rages, Orion ***debugs*** the ship's ***automation*** using his built-in ***actuator***. He hits a shiny red button and ***demolishes*** the engine's ***turbines***, destroying Dorn's only means of transportation!

As a young girl, Lucy would lie ***recumbent*** for hours ***pondering*** the Orion Colt series. Years later, she created her own comic book series about a time-travelling punk band, Abby and the Wildcats. But as Lucy's writing career blossomed, she heard about a ***kerfuffle*** between Gary Cohen, the creator of Orion Colt, and his manager. Sadly, Gary Cohen's manager ***bamboozled*** the writer out of all his money!

Lucy was ***befuddled*** by what to do next, but she ***abhorred*** the situation and had to help. Eventually, Lucy recommended that Gary receive a Lifetime Achievement Award for his contribution to comic books. Gary won the award and received a large cash prize. To thank Lucy for her help, he listed her as an ***honorary*** co-writer for his newest Orion Colt comic.

Ju

ly

1 JULY

Ephemeral

(ih-FEM-uh-rul)

lasting a very short time (adjective)

The queen of the night is a flowering cactus whose flowers grow from small stems to over 30 centimetres long and only bloom for a single night. The *ephemeral* flowers open at dusk and begin to wilt as soon as the sun hits them the following morning.

2 JULY

Intransigent

(in-TRANS-uh-juhnt)

refusing to compromise or abandon an extreme position or attitude (adjective)

Joseph Bazalgette was the chief engineer of the London sewer network in the mid-1800s. Original plans called for narrow tunnels, but the *intransigent* Bazalgette demanded that the tunnels be doubled in size in case of unforeseen circumstances. Thanks to his forward thinking, the sewer system was able to handle an unexpected population growth a hundred years later. The tunnels are still used today.

3 JULY

Lavation

(lav-AY-shuhn)

the act of washing or cleansing (noun)

In 2017, a company in Katy, Texas, USA, entered the world-record books as the longest car wash in the world. Vehicles move through numerous water sprayers and suds, 25 foam brushes and 17 blowers during the 77-metre-long *lavation*.

4 JULY

Bugbear

●●●●●●●●●●●●●

(BUG-bair)

something that makes someone feel overly worried or irritated (noun)

For many of us, spiders are a huge *bugbear*. They rarely hurt people and actually help us by catching and eating insects that can harm us. But according to some studies, up to 40 per cent of people surveyed are afraid of them.

Words at Work

Not sure what to be when you grow up? We've got you covered! Check out these working words and start learning the tools of the trade.

5 JULY

Animator

(AN-uh-may-tuh)

an artist who creates animated cartoons (noun)

Michiyo Yasuda was a Japanese *animator* who helped create award-winning cartoon films for Studio Ghibli and other film studios. She was known for her bold use of colour and received an Animation Lifetime Achievement Award at the Japanese Movie Critics Awards in 2011.

6 JULY

Cosmetologist

(koz-muh-TOL-uh-jist)

a person who offers beauty treatments for hair, skin and nails (noun)

Madam C. J. Walker is known as the first Black woman self-made millionaire in the United States. She made her fortune in the early 1900s as a successful *cosmetologist* who created hair and makeup products specifically for Black customers.

7 JULY

Aviator

(AY-vee-ay-tuh)

a person who flies aeroplanes or other types of aircraft (noun)

In 1932, Amelia Earhart became the first female *aviator* to fly solo across the Atlantic Ocean. It was one of many records she broke. Sadly, on her second attempt to circumnavigate the globe in 1937, Earhart's plane went missing over the Pacific Ocean. What happened to it is still a mystery.

8 JULY

Haberdasher

(HAB-uh-dash-uh)

someone who sells dressmaking and sewing goods (noun)

The City of London's Worshipful Company of *Haberdashers* began in the 14th century as a group of tradesmen working together to support their industry of selling small wares – including caps, pins, beads, purses and ribbons.

9 JULY

Entrepreneur

(on-truh-pruh-NER)

an individual who creates a new business and takes on financial risks in order to do so (noun)

In 1975, an American *entrepreneur* named Steve Jobs started brainstorming for a new computer company in his parents' garage. That company became Apple Inc, one of the most successful tech companies of all time. The family's house and garage were designated a Historical Resource in 2013 by the Los Altos Historical Commission in California, USA.

10 JULY

Volcanologist

(vol-kuh-NOL-uh-jist)

a scientist who studies volcanoes (noun)

Dr Keith Rowley is a *volcanologist* who studied volcanic eruptions in the Caribbean Islands and created safety plans for nearby communities. He went on to become the prime minister of Trinidad and Tobago.

11 JULY

Heyday

(HAY-day)

the time when someone or something is most successful, popular, etc. (noun)

The Little Tramp was a character created by British actor and filmmaker Charlie Chaplin. In the *heyday* of the silent film era, the character's signature bowler hat, cane, toothbrush moustache and silly charm became instantly recognisable and brought Chaplin worldwide fame.

12 JULY

Mausoleum

(maw-suh-LEE-uhm)

a large tomb (noun)

The *mausoleum* of Qin Shi Huang, the first emperor of China's Qin dynasty, is the country's largest preserved site. The burial site was discovered in 1974 when farmers found clay shards that led to the unearthing of the ancient tomb and thousands of life-size statues now known as the Terracotta Army.

13 JULY

Pizzazz

(puh-ZAZ)

a quality or style that is exciting and interesting (noun)

Elton John is a British singer-songwriter who started his career as a glam rocker in the early 1970s. His performances were full of *pizzazz*, and he became known for his theatrical style, energetic stage presence and flashy clothing, like rhinestone-encrusted sunglasses and suits with glitter-fringed trim.

14 JULY

Buff

●●●●●●●

(BUFF)

someone who has a keen interest in something and knows a lot about it (noun)

John Gale could be the United Kingdom's biggest film *buff*. He went to see his first film at the Swiss Cottage Odeon in London in 1945, at the age of five, and has been going back every week since. He is estimated to have watched over 7,000 films there, so many, in fact, that in 2015, the cinema gave him a free pair of tickets for every year he had been going.

15 JULY

Hypothesis

(hye-POTH-uh-suhss)

a possible explanation for an observed event (noun)

Since the 1800s, the city of Yoro, Honduras, has experienced an odd annual weather event where hundreds of fish rain down from the sky and on to the streets after severe thunderstorms. Some scientists have formed a *hypothesis* that the fish are transported into the air by a waterspout (a small column of rapidly swirling air in contact with a water surface). Another less exciting idea is that fish swimming in underground streams wash up on the street during heavy rains.

16 JULY

Marine

(muh-REEN)

of or relating to the sea or ocean (adjective)

An estimated 50–80 per cent of all life on Earth is *marine* life, with ocean covering over 70 per cent of the planet's surface. However, less than 20 per cent of that has been explored by humans. We know more about the surface of Mars than we do about the ocean floor.

17 JULY

Panacea

(pan-uh-SEE-uh)

something that will make everything about a situation better (noun)

Not long ago, diseases caused by bacteria, most of which are easily treated now, were major causes of death. In 1928, scientist Alexander Fleming discovered a mould that killed bacteria. He isolated the active ingredient, which proved to be the very first antibiotic medicine now known as penicillin, the groundbreaking *panacea* for bacterial infection.

18 JULY

Loggerheads

(LOG-uh-hedz)

in a state of strong disagreement – used in the phrase *at loggerheads* (noun)

In 2015, people around the world were at *loggerheads* over a picture of a dress from the Internet. While some people saw the dress as striped with black and blue, others saw it striped with gold and white. Experts say the disagreement may have been caused by how different people perceive colours.

19 JULY

Pulchritude

• • • • • • • • • • • • • •

(PUL-krih-tyood)

having a pleasing physical appearance (noun)

Oscar Wilde's novel *The Picture of Dorian Gray* is about a young man who becomes so obsessed with his own *pulchritude* that he trades his soul for eternal beauty. In the story, Dorian's portrait ages while he remains forever young and beautiful.

20 JULY

Akimbo

(uh-KIM-boh)

spread apart in a bent position (adjective)

Swimmer syndrome is a disease found in puppies and kittens that makes their limbs weak, causing them to splay out and often preventing the animal from standing or walking. Instead, afflicted animals will lie on their chest and try to move in a way that resembles a turtle swimming, its legs *akimbo*. Fortunately, physiotherapy can help, and the animal is usually able to attain normal movement as it grows.

Fruit

Take a big bite out of these juicy words!

21 JULY

Tamarind

(TAM-uh-rind)

the fruit of the tamarind tree, consisting of an oblong brown pod containing one to twelve flat seeds embedded in a brownish, sticky, acidic pulp (noun)

The *tamarind* tree is one of the most important food sources for Madagascar's ring-tailed lemurs. The lemurs eat both the leaves and fruit of the tree, which grow at different times of year and together provide nearly 50 per cent of their diet.

22 JULY

Durian

(DUR-ee-uhn)

a large, oval, tasty but foul-smelling fruit with a prickly rind (noun)

Due to its strong smell, *durian* is banned from public transportation in Thailand, Japan and Hong Kong.

23 JULY

Blackcurrant

(BLAK-kur-uhnt)

the small, edible dark purple berries of a European deciduous shrub (noun)

During World War II, shipments of citrus fruits to Great Britain nearly ground to a halt. Prime Minister Winston Churchill's government promoted the cultivation of *blackcurrant* bushes to keep citizens from getting scurvy. This native fruit is heavy in vitamin C, which prevents the deadly disease.

24 JULY

Quandong

(KWON-dong)

a red, round pitted fruit, similar to a peach, with a tart taste and large, edible seed that grows on shrubby trees in Australia (noun)

The *quandong* tree is a partially parasitic plant that attaches to the root systems of other plants and steals their nutrients.

25 JULY

Pitaya

(puh-TYE-uh)

a large red, yellow or pink oval fruit that has leathery skin with prominent scaly spikes and juicy flesh with many tiny black seeds native to Central and South America and Mexico (noun)

Pitaya is commonly called 'dragon fruit' in English due to its spiky exterior.

26 JULY

Opulent

●●●●●●●●●●●

(Op-yoo-luhnt)

very luxurious and expensive (adjective)

While most of France lived in poverty, King Louis XIV spent a great deal of taxpayer money in the 1600s to build the *opulent* Palace of Versailles. The palace features lavish gardens, fountains, a private zoo and more than 2,000 rooms.

27 JULY

Mulch

•••••••••

(MULCH)

a material (such as straw, leaves or small pieces of wood) that is spread over the ground in a garden to protect the plants, help them grow and stop weeds from sprouting (noun)

When trees die, many parts of the tree can be broken down and used for other purposes. Tree branches are often shredded into a nutrient-rich *mulch* that protects plants from the harsh winter elements.

28 JULY

Zeppelin

(ZEP-uh-lin)

a large aircraft without wings that floats because it is filled with gas and has a rigid frame inside its body to help keep its shape (noun)

When the Empire State Building was being built, investors announced that the building's height would be increased to allow *zeppelins* to dock at the very top. When the first zeppelin attempted this feat in 1931, it only docked for three minutes due to 64-kilometre-per-hour winds and caused a major traffic jam on the street below. The plan for zeppelin docking was eventually scrapped.

29 JULY

Minuscule

(MIN-uh-skyool)

very small (adjective)

Discovered in 2009, the smallest amphibian in the world is a frog that measures just 7 millimetres long. The creature is so *minuscule* that several could fit on the surface of a 5p coin. Named *Paedophryne amauensis*, it is the tiniest known animal with a backbone.

30 JULY

Karaoke

(kar-ee-OH-kee)

a form of entertainment in which a device plays the music of popular songs and people sing the words to the songs they choose (noun)

In Japanese, *karaoke* means 'empty orchestra'. In 1969, musician Daisuke Inoue had the inspiration for the karaoke machine when one of his clients asked him to create a backing track that he could sing along to. The portable machine, called the Juke-8, played eight song accompaniments and had a coin box. But Daisuke did not invent the word *karaoke*. The phrase is said to have originated when an orchestra went on strike, and the concert organisers played classical music through a machine.

31 JULY

Sprocket

(SPROK-uht)

a wheel that has a row of teeth around its edge which fit into the holes of something (such as a bicycle chain) and cause it to turn when the wheel turns (noun)

Before digital photography, everyone used cameras that took pictures on rolls of photosensitive film placed in the back of the camera. Many still use this type. Each film roll has holes along the sides which catch on a set of *sprockets* which are turned by operating a lever or button on the outside of the camera. After an image is captured, the film is advanced on the sprockets, until the roll has been used up and transferred from one side of the compartment to the other. Then the film can be removed and developed into photos.

Story of the Month

I have no idea what to be when I get older, and grown-ups make you choose too fast! I had an ***ephemeral*** career as 'class clown', but my teacher told me that doesn't count. I don't want to end up with a boring job, and I'm very ***intransigent*** about it. I want a career with ***pizzazz***!

Maybe I'll become a fruit ***entrepreneur*** who starts a business shipping fruit around the world! I'd travel to Australia to harvest ***quandong*** or trade ***pitaya*** and ***blackcurrant*** in Nigeria for fresh ***tamarind***. I'd even sell ***durian*** if I could put up with the smell. Maybe I could be a celebrity ***cosmetologist*** who gives a relaxing face ***lavation*** to actors before their close-ups. Or I could be the owner of a wild ***karaoke*** bar with guests singing and dancing, limbs all ***akimbo***. It would be great to be a cemetery caretaker, looking for ghosts in ***mausoleums*** and planting flowers in the ***mulch***. But perhaps I should become something more exciting, like a ***volcanologist*** studying an island lava flow from my ***marine*** vessel.

Sometimes I feel like I missed out on the ***heyday*** of certain jobs. I could have been an ***aviator*** of a ***zeppelin***, but no one really flies those anymore. I'm a bit of an old cartoon ***buff***, and would have loved to have been a Looney Tunes ***animator***. If I could go back in time, maybe I could have been a ***haberdasher*** of ***opulent*** clothes fit for a royal with ***pulchritude*** or a watchmaker carefully placing ***minuscule sprockets*** where they belong.

I can't seem to decide what to do when I grow up and it is becoming a bit of a ***bugbear***. My parents and I are at ***loggerheads*** over my future career. But why do I need a job at all? I have one ***hypothesis***. If we could live our lives and enjoy all of our passions, not just one, that would be quite the ***panacea***.

Aug

ust

1 AUGUST

Disperse

(dis-PERSS)

to distribute or spread widely (verb)

A rainbow appears when sunlight passes through raindrops and is *dispersed* into its full spectrum of colours, sending red, orange, yellow, green, blue, indigo and violet light into the sky.

2 AUGUST

Taboo

(tuh-BOO)

not acceptable to talk about or do (adjective)

Judy Blume's novel *Are You There God? It's Me, Margaret* has been adored by readers around the world for decades. Published in 1970, the story includes subjects that many adults considered *taboo* at the time, such as puberty, buying bras and interfaith marriage. Despite being banned by many libraries in the United States, the book went on to become a modern classic.

3 AUGUST

Accumulate

(uh-KYOO-myuh-layt)

to gather or acquire something gradually as time passes (verb)

Mansa Musa was a 14th-century ruler of the kingdom of Mali, which was at its peak the largest and richest empire in West African history. Musa *accumulated* so much wealth that he crashed the Egyptian economy for 12 years after visiting the country and paying for things with solid gold.

4 AUGUST

Killjoy

●●●●●●●●●

(KIL-joy)

a person who spoils other people's fun or enjoyment (noun)

Oliver Cromwell, who ruled the British Isles as Lord Protector in the 1650s, was a strict Puritan. Some thought him a *killjoy* because he did not approve of Christmas celebrations. During his rule, soldiers were sent through the city to seize and destroy any special food prepared for the festivities.

5 AUGUST

Monopoly

(muh-NOP-uh-lee)

complete control of all goods and services in a particular market (noun)

Marcus Licinius Crassus was an ancient Roman general and politician who made his wealth in many dishonest ways. He gained a *monopoly* on firefighting services in Rome and used his power to make homeowners pay him huge bribes. If they refused to pay, Crassus would let their houses burn down.

6 AUGUST

Ambidextrous

(am-bih-DEK-struhss)

able to use the right and left hands equally well (adjective)

Very few people – about 1 per cent of the population – are born *ambidextrous*. Still, the ability to use both hands equally well can be learned over time. In a 1919 article, Serbian inventor Nikola Tesla wrote, 'I am ambidextrous now', though he admitted to being born left-handed.

Bugs

Don't let these creepy, crawly words get under your skin.

7 AUGUST

Cicada

(sih-KAH-duh)

a species of large black insects with long, transparent wings, of which the males have a loud mating call (noun)

Some species of *cicada* stay underground for 13 to 17 years before maturing into adulthood and emerging all at once in a large group called a 'brood'.

8 AUGUST

Botfly

(BOT-flye)

a small, hairy fly that lays eggs inside the bodies of large mammals (noun)

When *botflies* lay eggs in the nostrils of sheep, they can cause a nervous condition called 'blind staggers', where the host animal walks with uneven steps and appears to be blind.

9 AUGUST

Millipede

(MIL-uh-peed)

an invertebrate animal with a long body composed of many segments, most of which have two pairs of legs (noun)

Millipedes are born with only a few pairs of legs and grow many more pairs during their lifetime. One adult species of white millipede from California, USA, boasts up to 750 legs.

10 AUGUST

Katydid

(KAY-tee-did)

a large green grasshopper usually with organs on the forewings of the males that produce a loud shrill sound (noun)

Male *katydids* attract females by rubbing their forewings together to create chirping noises. While it may sound like they 'sing' in unison, scientists have learned that each male is trying to be the first to sing a new note. Studies have shown that female katydids select the first male in a group that broadcasts a new tone, even if it was only 70 milliseconds faster than the other males.

11 AUGUST

Weevil

(WEE-vuhl)

a small beetle with an elongated snout (noun)

There are more than 60,000 species of *weevil* in the world. Weevils are herbivores that often feed on the same plant species their entire lives. Many weevils are named after the foods they eat, including the rice weevil and the grain weevil.

12 AUGUST

Mantis

(MAN-tuhss)

a large green insect that feeds on other insects and holds its prey in its forelimbs (noun)

This formidable bug is often called a 'praying *mantis*' because it appears to draw its limbs together in prayer when it latches on to prey. But mantises are not saintly insects. Female mantises are known to kill and eat their male partners.

13 AUGUST

Aardvark

(AHRD-vahrk)

a large African animal with a long nose that eats ants and other insects using its elongated tongue (noun)

The *aardvark* is revered by several African tribes, including the Mangbetu, who admire it for its bravery. Some people wear aardvark teeth on bracelets to serve as good luck charms.

14 AUGUST

Odoriferous

(oh-duh-RIF-uh-russ)

strong-smelling (adjective)

Scientists conducted a study where they played different kinds of music to cheese as it aged. A panel of judges found that cheese exposed to hip-hop music was more *odoriferous* than cheese exposed to classical, rock or techno music.

15 AUGUST

Igloo

(IG-loo)

a temporary winter dwelling made of blocks of snow or ice in the form of a dome (noun)

Despite being cold, snow is actually a great insulator of heat. Even if temperatures outside drop as low as -40 degrees Celsius, inside an *igloo*, body heat can keep the temperature as high as 16 degrees Celsius.

16 AUGUST

Abacus

• • • • • • • • • •

(AB-uh-kuhss)

a device used for counting and calculating by sliding small balls or beads along rods or in grooves (noun)

The average *abacus* can easily fit on a tabletop, but Ajit Singh from India decided to make one that was much, much larger. In 2011, Ajit built an abacus that measured 6.8 metres by 3.2 metres and weighed 119 kilograms, the largest one in existence.

17 AUGUST

Camouflage

(KAM-uh-flahzh)

something (such as colour or shape) that makes an animal difficult to see in the area around it (noun)

Chameleons are masters of the art of changing colour, but the vivid colours they produce are rarely used as *camouflage*. While chameleons adjust their colours slightly to match their backgrounds, elaborate displays of colour are reserved for attracting mates and defending their territory.

18 AUGUST

Odyssey

(OD-uh-see)

a long journey full of adventures (noun)

Inspired by Jules Verne's novel *Around the World in 80 Days*, journalist Nellie Bly undertook an *odyssey* in 1889 to travel around the world in even less time. Bly travelled alone by ship, train, horse, donkey and rickshaw, and she made it around the world in only 72 days.

19 AUGUST

Fortnight

(FORT-nyte)

a period of 14 days: two weeks (noun)

Pope Urban VII was Pope of the Roman Catholic Church in 1590 for less than a *fortnight*. He died of malaria just 12 days after becoming pope, making it the shortest reign in the history of the Church.

20 AUGUST

Chitchat

(CHIT-chat)

friendly conversation about things that are not very important (noun)

Small talk, like discussing the weather or weekend plans, can be an important social tool. Not only does *chitchat* make people happier, but it can also deepen connections, build trust and increase the ability to solve problems.

21 AUGUST

Comeuppance

(kum-UP-uhnss)

punishment that someone deserves to receive (noun)

In *The Twits* by Roald Dahl, evil pranksters Mr and Mrs Twit set traps for birds so they can make them into pies. They get their *comeuppance*, though, when the birds play a trick back on them which sees the couple glue their own heads to the floor. Stuck upside-down, they shrink into the floorboards until nothing is left of them.

22 AUGUST

Pareidolia

(par-ih-DOL-ee-uh)

the tendency to see a specific or meaningful image in a random visual pattern (noun)

Pedra da Gávea is an 844-metre-high mountain in Brazil's Tijuca Forest. Because of *pareidolia*, some people say they can see a person's face, complete with a hat or helmet, in the large rock at the peak.

Space Words

Blast off to another galaxy with these galactic words!

23 AUGUST

Asteroid

(ASS-tuh-royd)

a small, rocky object that orbits the Sun (noun)

On 25 November 2005, JAXA (Japan Aerospace Exploration Agency) landed the Hayabusa spacecraft on the *asteroid* Itokawa. It was the first space mission to collect surface material from an asteroid and bring it back to Earth.

24 AUGUST

Gibbous

(GIB-uhss)

with more than half but not all of the apparent disc illuminated – used to describe a view of the Moon or a planet (adjective)

As the Moon orbits the Earth, the parts of the Moon that face the Sun are illuminated. When more than half the Moon faces the Sun, it creates a *gibbous* moon, which occurs right before and after a full moon.

25 AUGUST

Extraterrestrial

(ek-struh-tuh-RESS-tree-uhl)

coming from or existing outside the planet Earth (adjective)

The first interstellar object to pass through our solar system was spotted in 2017 by astronomers in Hawaii, who named it ʻOumuamua. Some astronomers believe the object to be a piece of rock that broke away from a planet, but there are a few who think that it may have been an *extraterrestrial* visitor from an alien civilisation.

26 AUGUST

Lunar

(LOO-nuhr)

of, or related to, the Moon (adjective)

NASA astronaut Harrison Schmitt was a part of the Apollo 17 mission that landed on the Moon on 11 December 1972. As he and a fellow astronaut explored the Moon's surface, dust stuck to their boots, suits and tools. When Schmitt returned to the spacecraft, he removed his helmet and his nose got stuffed up. That's how he discovered he was allergic to *lunar* dust.

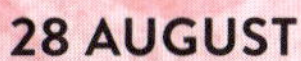

27 AUGUST

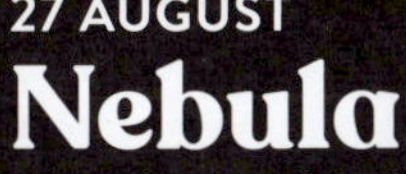

Nebula

(NEB-yoo-luh)

a large cloud of gas or dust in outer space (noun)

The closest *nebula* to Earth, the Helix Nebula, is made of gas given off by a dying star.

28 AUGUST

Supernova

(SOO-puh-NOH-vuh)

the bright explosion of a star at the end of its life that can be one billion times brighter than the Sun (noun)

Some heavy elements, like iron, are only created in *supernovas*. Humans typically have between 3 and 4 grams of iron in their bodies, which means we all carry the remains of space explosions.

29 AUGUST

Deciduous

(dih-SIH-joo-uhss)

having leaves that fall off every year (adjective)

Deciduous trees prepare for winter hibernation by shutting down their food production systems and reducing the amount of chlorophyll in their leaves. Chlorophyll is a chemical that helps plants make food and gives them their green colour. When trees reduce the amount of chlorophyll, other chemicals become more noticeable, and this is what gives autumn leaves their red, orange and yellow colours.

30 AUGUST

Phenomenon

(fih-NO-muh-nuhn)

an exceptional, unusual or abnormal person, thing or occurrence (noun)

Under the right conditions, Horsetail Falls in Yosemite National Park in the United States gives off a glow resembling lava or falling fire, a natural *phenomenon* referred to as 'firefall'.

31 AUGUST

Temerity

(tih-MEH-rih-tee)

unreasonable confidence or boldness (noun)

Kitty O'Neil was a Hollywood stuntwoman known for holding a land-speed record of 825 kilometres per hour while driving a three-wheeled rocket through the desert. Her *temerity* allowed her to succeed at death-defying stunts and earned her the title of 'the fastest woman in the world'.

Story of the Month

Captain's log: Day 4,852 – It has been a ***fortnight*** since my last log. Our spaceship is nearing the end of its long ***odyssey*** after passing through an ***asteroid*** field to arrive above a new planet. Let me just say, we have ***accumulated*** some unusual observations. We have seen ***gibbous lunar*** views and an explosive ***supernova***. We even saw a ***nebula*** that looked like an ***igloo***, but it may have just been my own ***pareidolia***.

Meanwhile, the crew is engaging in careless ***chitchat*** and losing focus while on duty. I don't want to be a ***killjoy***, nor do I want fun to be ***taboo*** on the ship, but we must remain committed to the mission. I have had to reprimand the crew many times. I would rather their ***comeuppance*** be a stern warning from me than the breakdown of our ship. ***Temerity*** in space could lead to disaster. We are carrying precious living cargo from Earth, including ***cicadas***, ***botflies***, ***weevils***, ***mantises*** and ***katydids***. We also have larger creatures, like ***aardvarks***, which always try to eat the insects. I need my crew to focus and keep these animals safe. They are supposed to be experts in zoology and astrophysics, but I doubt my crew could even use a simple ***abacus***.

Now for the most exciting discovery – I am stunned at a ***phenomenon*** taking place on the planet below our spaceship. Here, we have discovered ***extraterrestrial*** life! In addition to ***odoriferous*** plants and ***deciduous*** trees, we found an insect-like creature that ***disperses*** an acidic gas every few days. It looks like a ***millipede*** with hundreds of small legs and two giant ***ambidextrous*** arms it uses to hunt prey. This morning, we discovered that the creature uses ***camouflage*** to blend into its surroundings. It also appears to have a ***monopoly*** on the planet's mushroom population – every mushroom we can see is hollowed out to make room for the creature's eggs. I wonder if this little creature is intelligent enough to communicate. We will have to wait and see. Until next time...

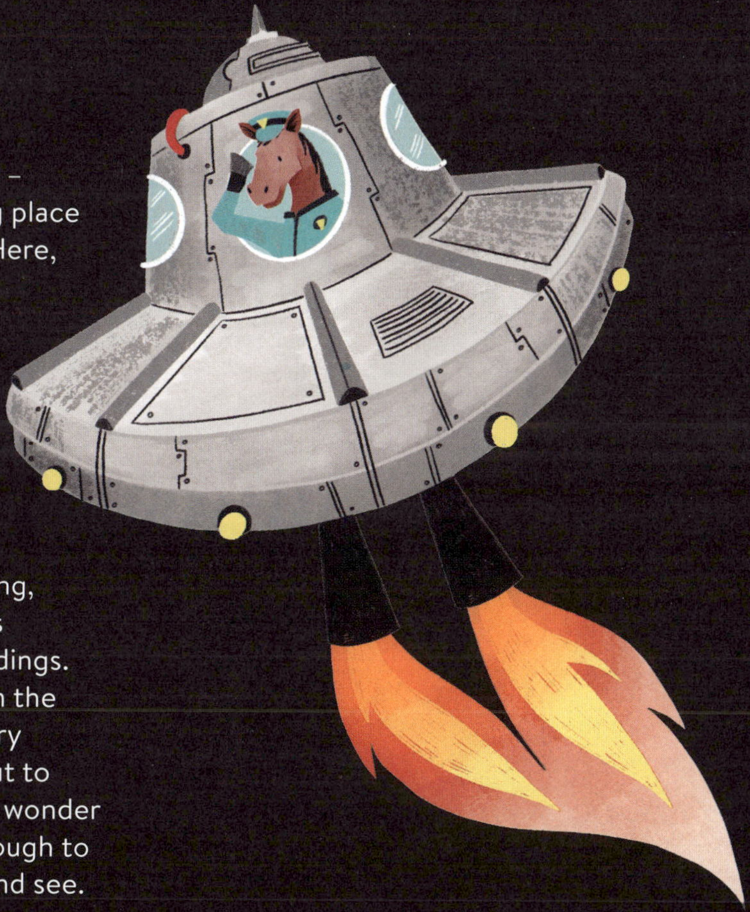

Sept

ember

1 SEPTEMBER

Cuckoo

(KUH-koo)

a type of bird that lays its eggs in the nests of other birds and has a call that sounds like its name (noun)

To chime the hour, a *cuckoo* clock opens a small wooden door, and a wooden cuckoo emerges to cry 'cuckoo' once for one o'clock, twice for two o'clock, and so on. It is thought that these clocks were originally made in the 1600s with wood from the Black Forest in southwest Germany.

2 SEPTEMBER

Ostentatious

(oss-tuhn-TAY-shuhss)

attracting attention, admiration or envy in an obvious way (adjective)

The Sultan of Brunei, Hassanal Bolkiah, has a collection of approximately 7,000 cars, including an *ostentatious* Rolls-Royce Silver Spur II stretch limousine. The entire vehicle is plated with 24-carat gold and has an estimated price of £10 million.

3 SEPTEMBER

Trajectory

(truh-JEK-tuh-ree)

the curved path an object follows as it moves through the air or through space (noun)

Players of ball sports have to learn how to control the *trajectory* of the ball. The main factors that determine a ball's flight path are the angle and speed at which it is hit or thrown and the size and weight of the ball itself.

4 SEPTEMBER

Unique

(yoo-NEEK)

being the only one of its kind (adjective)

Everyone knows that no two persons' fingerprints are the same, but few people are aware that scientists have discovered the same for tongue prints. Every person has a *unique* pattern on their tongue.

5 SEPTEMBER

Regenerate

(rih-JEN-uh-rayt)

to grow again after being lost or damaged (verb)

Of all the organs in a human body, the liver is the only one that has the incredible ability to *regenerate*. If 25 to 65 per cent of the liver is damaged or removed, the organ can fully grow back to its original size.

6 SEPTEMBER

Cornucopia

(kaw-nyoo-KOH-pee-uh)

a container that is shaped like a horn and is full of fruit and vegetables; a great amount or source of something (noun)

Across cultures, the *cornucopia* has become a symbol of abundance and the harvest season and is also known as the 'horn of plenty'. The ancient Greeks believed the horn was broken off the head of a baby goat and used to feed Zeus, the king of their gods, by his nurse when he was a baby. According to legend, an endless supply of nourishment flowed from the broken horn, giving it its name.

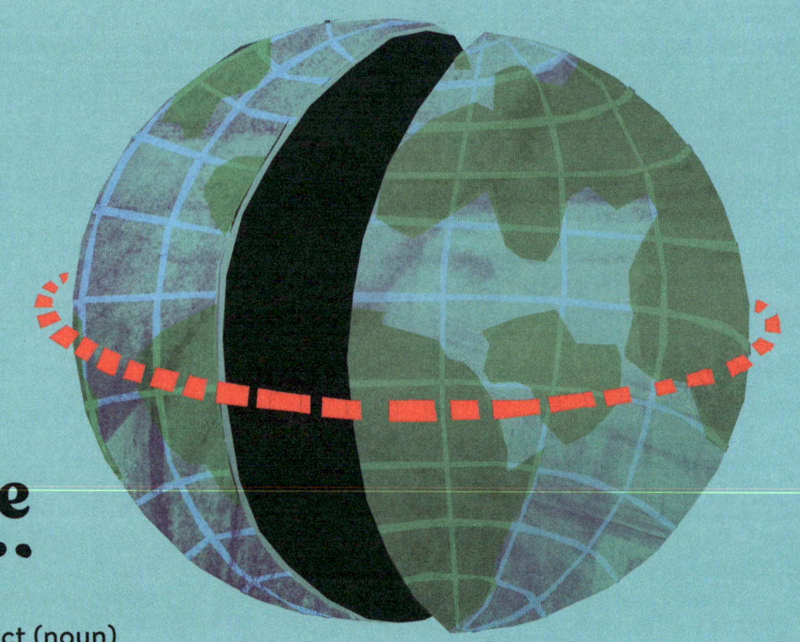

7 SEPTEMBER

Hemisphere

(HEM-uh-sfeer)

half of a sphere or round object (noun)

The Earth can be divided into *hemispheres* in two different ways: vertically and horizontally. The equator divides Earth horizontally into the northern and southern hemispheres. The prime meridian divides Earth vertically into eastern and western hemispheres. Africa is the only continent in the world that crosses both the equator and the prime meridian, meaning it rests on all four areas of the Earth – east, west, north and south.

8 SEPTEMBER

Quid pro quo

●●●●●●●●●●●●●●●●●●●●

(KWID-proh-KWOH)

something that is given to you or done for you in return for something you have given or done for someone else (noun)

The relationship between chimpanzees and the African nutmeg plant involves something of a *quid pro quo*. Chimps eat the nutmeg to calm stomach aches. As the seed of the nutmeg plant moves through a chimp's body, the tough outer layer is stripped away by stomach acids. When chimps pass the seed in their stool, it can grow into a new tree because the outer layer has been removed.

9 SEPTEMBER

Juggernaut

(JUG-uh-nawt)

something (such as a force, campaign or movement) that is extremely large and powerful and cannot be stopped (noun)

In 1780, a *juggernaut* of a hurricane called the Great Hurricane of 1780 roared over the Atlantic Ocean and the Caribbean Islands. Survivors in Barbados and Saint Lucia claimed that the winds were so strong they blew over sturdy stone buildings and entire forts.

10 SEPTEMBER

Agenda

(uh-JEN-duh)

a list of things to be considered or done (noun)

German composer Ludwig van Beethoven often kept to the same daily schedule. After getting up at dawn, his *agenda* consisted of carefully counting sixty beans for his cup of coffee and working for several hours. In the afternoon he would usually go for a long walk outdoors, with a pencil and sheet of music paper in his pocket to note down any sudden ideas. In the evening, he might read a newspaper at a tavern or spend time with friends. He was in bed by 10:00 PM, ready to do it again the next day.

11 SEPTEMBER

Crochet

(KROH-shay)

a method of making cloth or clothing by using a needle with a hook at the end to form yarn into interwoven loops (noun)

Polish artist Olek often uses *crochet* to create site-specific works of art. Olek travels across the world creating giant yarn 'cosies' that cover buildings and large monuments. She once covered an entire house in Sweden with pink crocheted fabric and crocheted a head-to-toe jumper for the Charging Bull statue in New York City's financial capital, Wall Street.

12 SEPTEMBER

Adjacent

(uh-JAY-sunt)

close or near; sharing a border, wall or point (adjective)

In 2019, archaeologists discovered the remains of a board game from 1,800 years ago near the site of an ancient Roman bathhouse. Oddly, the board game was being used as a floorboard in an *adjacent* building. Historians believe that someone at the bathhouse broke the board game, and the broken pieces were used to build the floor of a nearby structure.

Vivid Vocabulary

Brighten your world by swapping common colours for these handsome hues.

13 SEPTEMBER

Cerulean

(suh-ROO-lee-uhn)

a blue colour, like the sky or the sea (noun)

In 2000, the colour and graphic company Pantone chose *cerulean* as its 'Colour of the Year'. The company called the colour 'tranquil' and 'peaceful'.

14 SEPTEMBER

Puce

(PYOOSS)

a dark red (noun)

In 18th-century France, *puce*-coloured clothing became fashionable in the court of Louis XVI. The brownish-red colour kept clothes from showing much dirt and grime, which allowed royals to look their best.

15 SEPTEMBER

Flaxen

(FLAK-suhn)

resembling the pale, soft straw colour of flax plant fibres (adjective)

In Charles Dickens's book *David Copperfield*, the title character describes his attraction to a young girl 'with a round face and curly *flaxen* hair'.

16 SEPTEMBER

Cyan

(SYE-an)

a greenish-blue colour (noun)

Cyan is one of the main colours of ink used in printing, along with black, yellow and magenta. When combined, these four inks can create the thousands of colours you find in books and magazines.

17 SEPTEMBER

Periwinkle

(PEH-rih-wing-kuhl)

a pale colour somewhere between blue and violet (noun)

Periwinkle was a common colour in ancient Egyptian jewellery, often made from a bluish, purplish stone called lapis lazuli.

18 SEPTEMBER

Chartreuse

(shahr-TRERZ)

a bright yellow-green colour (noun)

According to legend, the colour *chartreuse* is named after a bright green drink created by a 16th-century alchemist who promised good health and a long life to those who drank it.

19 SEPTEMBER

Dilute

(dye-LYOOT)

to lessen the strength of something by mixing it with something else (verb)

In the 1600s, the bubonic plague killed about 15 to 20 per cent of London's population. Doctors believed people caught the disease by breathing in deadly gases, so they tried to *dilute* the bad air with something just as strong to prevent people from getting sick. They advised patients to trap any gas they passed in containers and have these 'fart jars' ready to sniff in case they were exposed to plague-filled air. (The plague was actually spread by biting fleas.)

20 SEPTEMBER

Tittle-tattle

(TIT-uhl-TAT-uhl)

talk or stories about someone that may not always be true (noun)

In 1692, Salem, Massachusetts, USA, was swept up in hysteria as townsfolk accused one another of practising witchcraft, sparking a series of court cases known as the Salem Witch Trials. In court, tests were performed to determine if people were witches, such as checking the accused for moles that were considered 'witches' marks'. Unsupported gossip and *tittle-tattle* were also permitted as evidence, and ultimately 19 people were executed before the community came to its senses.

21 SEPTEMBER

Contentious

(con-TEN-shuhss)

likely to cause disagreement and arguments (adjective)

Major football competitions have introduced video technology to reduce the number of *contentious* decisions made during matches. In addition to the referees on the field, a video assistant referee, or VAR, watches camera feeds from a booth and can help officials to review any play that might be in doubt.

22 SEPTEMBER

Contented

(kon-TEN-tihd)

happy and satisfied; showing or feeling contentment (adjective)

When cats are *contented*, they often make a low, vibrating sound called purring. Scientists are still not sure how cats produce a purr. But they've found that some larger cats, like cheetahs and bobcats, also make a purring sound.

23 SEPTEMBER

Inflation

(in-FLAY-shuhn)

a continual increase in the price of goods and services (noun)

In 1920s Germany, *inflation* became so bad that in some restaurants, waiters would stand on chairs every half hour and announce the new prices for their menu. There were reports of people sitting down to order a meal and finding that the price had shot up by the time the bill arrived.

24 SEPTEMBER

Perspire

(puh-SPYRE)

to sweat through the pores as a result of heat, stress or physical exertion (verb)

Sweating is the body's way of regulating temperature. When you *perspire*, the moisture on your skin evaporates, which cools the skin. The average person has two to four million sweat glands on their body.

25 SEPTEMBER

Predict

(pruh-DIKT)

to say that something will happen in the future (verb)

Neptune was the first planet to be discovered using mathematics. Working separately, astronomers John Couch Adams and Urbain-Jean-Joseph Le Verrier each noticed that the planet Uranus was being pulled slightly off its normal orbit and guessed that the cause was an undiscovered planet. With some calculations, they figured out the planet's location and size. A short time later, astronomer Johann Gottfried Galle pointed his telescope at the spot Adams and Le Verrier had pinpointed. And there was Neptune, right where they had *predicted* it would be!

26 SEPTEMBER

Juxtapose

(JUK-stuh-pohz)

to place (different things) together in order to create an interesting effect or to show how they are the same or different (verb)

When people *juxtapose* two things that are very different, they often say it's like 'comparing apples and oranges'. However, apples and oranges are both edible fruit that contain vitamin C and similar amounts of calories. In most cases, juxtaposing two unlike things is more like comparing apples and helicopters.

27 SEPTEMBER

Rustic

(RUSS-tik)

made in a simple style, often from rough wood (adjective)

Tove Jansson, creator of the Moomin books, would spend her summers in a *rustic* wooden cabin on a tiny rocky island far out in the archipelago of the Gulf of Finland. Her love of the outdoors and a simple life, and her understanding of nature's often brutal power, can be seen throughout her work.

28 SEPTEMBER

Spurn

(SPERN)

to refuse to accept someone or something that you do not think deserves your respect, attention or affection (verb)

Shakespeare's Romeo wasn't lucky in love. He met Juliet at a party he was urged to go to because he had been *spurned* by another girl, Rosaline. The idea was that when he saw all the other beautiful women there, he would quickly get over Rosaline. Which is precisely what happened, except that his new love affair didn't go too well either.

29 SEPTEMBER

Kerplunk

(kuh-PLUNK)

the sound of something landing noisily (noun)

Legend has it that the young Sir Isaac Newton first came up with his law of gravity when an apple fell from a tree and hit him on the head, *kerplunk*! (It is true that Newton was inspired by observing the way apples in his garden fell straight down to Earth from the trees, but there's no evidence he was ever hit by one!)

30 SEPTEMBER

Conclave

(KON-klayv)

a private or secret meeting or group (noun)

The Hermetic Order of the Golden Dawn was a *conclave* devoted to the study and practice of all things weird and spooky. It was set up in 1888 to provide a social platform for those interested in ritual magic but fell apart 12 years later due to disagreements between its senior members. Some notable people were members of the conclave, including Bram Stoker, *Dracula* author, Edith Nesbit, children's author, Florence Farr, a leading actress of the day, and Irish poet W.B. Yeats.

Story of the Month

The Superminati is a ***conclave*** of the world's greatest superheroes. Their meetings are a secret to all except the superheroes and located deep in a jungle that could make even the fittest ***perspire***. From the outside, the headquarters of the Superminati looks like a hermit's hut. But ***juxtaposed*** with that ***rustic*** exterior is the inside – a strangely large, futuristic space with a ***cornucopia*** of high-tech screens, computers, gadgets and devices.

When all are in attendance, the room is filled with bright and colourful costumes bordering on ***ostentatious***. There are caped crusaders dressed in every shade, including ***cerulean***, ***cyan***, ***puce***, ***chartreuse*** and ***periwinkle***. Volatus, who can chart a perfectly accurate ***trajectory*** that carries him across entire ***hemispheres*** in just minutes, is usually in attendance, along with Regina Tiv, who has the ***unique*** power of ***regenerating*** parts of her body. And then there's Zip – a super-fast, super-strong ***juggernaut*** of a person, capable of running on water. As you can imagine, the behind-the-scenes ***tittle-tattle*** is always very entertaining.

As the heroes have made the world safer, however, the ***agenda*** for the Superminati has become ***diluted*** with 'boring' problems like ***inflation*** and political ***quid pro quos***. In this year's meeting some members even fell asleep during the first presentation.

But the quiet didn't last long. Seemingly from nowhere, a ***cuckoo*** sound interrupted the meeting. Then another. And another. And many, many more. Where could it have been coming from? After all, the headquarters was sealed. Someone in the room must have been to blame.

Contentious accusations came thick and fast. Heroes began pointing the finger at one another and ***spurned*** each other's claims of innocence. Finally, a voice called out and the fighting stopped. In the corner, ***crocheting*** with ***flaxen*** wool, sat Futura, a superhero with the power to ***predict*** the future. She spoke calmly, saying, 'Zip, open the cabinet ***adjacent*** to your chair.' He did. And what do you think happened? That's right, a cuckoo clock fell out, ***kerplunk***, and the noise stopped. 'Thank goodness that's over,' said a ***contented*** Futura. She picked up her wool. 'Let's continue the meeting.'

Oct

ober

1 OCTOBER

Ignite

(ig-NYTE)

to set on fire or cause a fuel to burn (verb)

Did you know that most cars on the road have a fire burning inside them? A petrol-powered engine mixes fuel with oxygen and *ignites* the mixture with a device called a spark plug. By controlling the amount of oxygen in the mixture, the engine can capture the energy from the burning fuel to make the car go and still keep the fire under control so it doesn't engulf the car.

2 OCTOBER

Acupuncture

(AK-yoo-punk-chuh)

a method of treating pain or illness by placing needles into a person's skin at particular points on the body (noun)

In traditional medicine in China, where *acupuncture* originated, the technique is used to help balance one's 'Chi' (life force or flow of energy). The inserted needles are meant to redirect the flow of energy through proper pathways. Scientists have studied acupuncture, and many believe that it can relieve pain because the needles help stimulate muscles and nerves in a way that boosts the body's natural painkillers.

3 OCTOBER

Vice versa

(VYCE-VER-suh)

used to say that the opposite of a statement is also true (adverb)

Miyamoto Musashi and Sasaki Kojirō were two legendary Japanese swordsmen in the 1600s. Musashi saw Kojirō as a threat and *vice versa*, so they agreed to duel it out on an island. Musashi arrived late to annoy Kojirō and turned up with a wooden sword carved from an oar. Kojirō attacked first in anger but was swiftly dealt a fatal blow.

4 OCTOBER

Slapstick

(SLAP-stik)

comedy that involves physical action (such as falling down or hitting people) (noun)

Laurel and Hardy were a comedy duo that performed *slapstick* in the early to mid 1900s. They were masters of physical comedy, be it fighting, dancing or gags involving props. In *The Music Box*, one of their best-loved short films, they play delivery men trying to carry a piano up a long set of steps, with hilarious consequences.

5 OCTOBER

Schmooze

(SHMOOZ)

to talk with someone in a friendly way, often in order to get some advantage for yourself (verb)

In 2020, Hungarian artist Andi Schmied posed as a billionaire and *schmoozed* estate agents to gain access to some of New York City's most elite penthouses. She brought a camera with her to photograph views from the luxury apartments and turned those pictures into a book.

6 OCTOBER

Alter

•••••••

(AWL-tuh)

to change partly but not completely (verb)

In 2020, Princess Beatrice married Edoardo Mapelli Mozzi in a gown that had been previously worn by her grandmother, Queen Elizabeth II. The dress was *altered* to fit Beatrice and large puffy sleeves were added.

Musical Words

The notes on a written sheet of music tell a musician what to play. These musical words tell a musician exactly how to play a piece of music.

7 OCTOBER

Crescendo

(kruh-SHEN-doh)

a gradual increase in loudness (noun)

The abbreviation 'cresc.' or an elongated angle bracket (<) written in sheet music tells musicians to play gradually louder for a *crescendo*.

8 OCTOBER

Fortissimo

(for-TISS-uh-moh)

very loud or very loudly (adjective; adverb)

When two letter f's (ff) appear in sheet music, musicians play *fortissimo*.

9 OCTOBER

Pianissimo

(pee-uh-NISS-uh-moh)

very soft or very softly (adjective; adverb)

Two letter p's (pp) tell musicians to play *pianissimo*.

10 OCTOBER

Staccato

(stuh-KAH-toh)

in a manner that keeps the musical notes short and separate from one another (adverb; adjective)

When a dot appears above or below a note, it means the note is *staccato*.

11 OCTOBER

Legato

(lih-GAH-toh)

in a smooth and connected manner (adverb; adjective)

A curved line above or below a row of notes tells the musician to play *legato*, blending those notes into one another.

12 OCTOBER

Superfluous

(soo-PER-floo-uhss)

beyond what is needed; not necessary (adjective)

A vast collection of ocean debris known as the Great Pacific Garbage Patch floats in the North Pacific Ocean. Debris builds over time because humans produce *superfluous* amounts of single-use plastics. Scientists agree that eliminating our use of disposable plastics and switching to biodegradable resources is the best way to keep the mess from getting even bigger.

13 OCTOBER

Mangle

(MANG-uhl)

to injure or damage (something or someone) severely by tearing or crushing (verb)

In 1986, a canvas by abstract painter Barnett Newman called 'Who's Afraid of Red, Yellow and Blue III' was shown at the Stedelijk Museum in Amsterdam, the Netherlands. The painting of bold colours and straight lines upset many in the art world who felt that Newman's art was so simple, anyone could paint it. One angry person even *mangled* the painting by slashing it with a blade.

14 OCTOBER

Scholar

(SKOL-uh)

a person who devotes their life to study (noun)

The Islamic Golden Age was a period of great advancement in medicine, technology, mathematics and culture from the 18th to 13th centuries. With a high value placed on education, *scholars* were encouraged to acquire knowledge in many fields of study.

15 OCTOBER

Whodunnit

(hoo-DUN-it)

a novel, play or movie about a murder where the audience is given clues to the identity of the murderer but doesn't find out for sure until the end (noun)

Agatha Christie wrote over 66 detective novels in her life and is often considered a master of the *whodunnit*. She was once at the centre of her own mystery, as well, when she disappeared for 11 days after her first husband asked for a divorce. The story made the front page of newspapers and caused thousands of volunteers to try and find her, eventually leading to her discovery in a hotel.

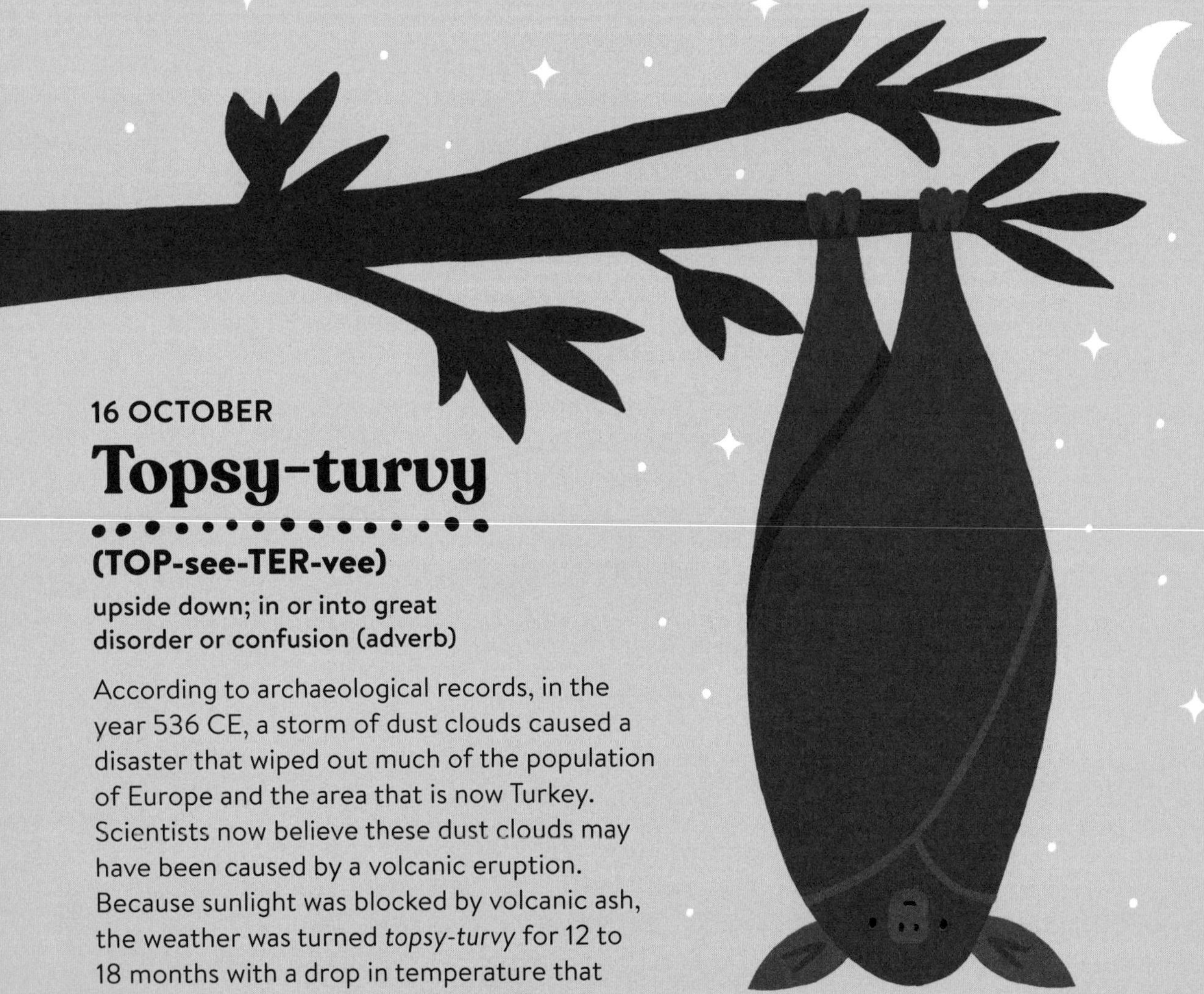

16 OCTOBER

Topsy-turvy

(TOP-see-TER-vee)

upside down; in or into great disorder or confusion (adverb)

According to archaeological records, in the year 536 CE, a storm of dust clouds caused a disaster that wiped out much of the population of Europe and the area that is now Turkey. Scientists now believe these dust clouds may have been caused by a volcanic eruption. Because sunlight was blocked by volcanic ash, the weather was turned *topsy-turvy* for 12 to 18 months with a drop in temperature that resulted in icy summers and severe winters.

17 OCTOBER

Derive

(dih-RYVE)

to take or get from a source (verb)

While modern marshmallows are made from sugar, glucose syrup and gelatin, thousands of years ago they were *derived* from the mallow plant that grows wild in marshes. Some of the first people to enjoy the gooey treat were ancient Egyptians, but back then it was rare and reserved for gods and royalty.

18 OCTOBER

Pugnacious

(pug-NAY-shuhss)

showing a readiness or desire to fight or argue (adjective)

Humans are unusual among animals partly because we can think logically. Recently, French scientists put forth a theory called the 'argumentative theory of reasoning'. It states that our ability to reason evolved to win arguments. This means that our ability to think logically may be a new version of an old need to win fights with other *pugnacious* people.

19 OCTOBER

Cantankerous

(kan-TANG-kuh-ruhs)

easily annoyed, argumentative and complaining (adjective)

In Sandra Cisneros's 2002 novel *Caramelo*, the character of Soledad is known as the 'Awful Grandmother' because of her *cantankerous* nature. She is always criticising her family, and even tells her granddaughter Celaya off for laughing too hard.

20 OCTOBER

Mnemonic

(nih-MON-ik)

something (such as a word, a sentence or a song) that helps people remember something else (such as a rule or a list of names) (noun)

A *mnemonic* can be a useful trick for remembering the planets in our solar system in the order of their distance from the Sun. The first letters of every word in the sentence '**M**y **V**ery **E**xcellent **M**other **J**ust **S**erved **U**s **N**uggets' match the first letters of planets **M**ercury, **V**enus, **E**arth, **M**ars, **J**upiter, **S**aturn, **U**ranus and **N**eptune.

21 OCTOBER

Rickety

(RIK-uh-tee)

weak or unstable and likely to break (adjective)

In 1998, a marble bust made by French artist Edmé Bouchardon in 1728 was discovered in a *rickety* shed on an industrial park in Scotland. The bust of Sir John Gordon, valued at almost £1.5 million, was found being used as a door stop. It has since been restored and shown in museums around the world.

22 OCTOBER

Edible

(ED-uh-buhl)

able to be eaten (adjective)

Archaeologists have discovered pots of honey in ancient Egyptian tombs that have remained unspoiled. If honey stays completely sealed, it can last for thousands of years and still be *edible*!

23 OCTOBER

Malaise

(mah-LAYZ)

a slight or general feeling of not being healthy or happy (noun)

In addition to a stuffy nose, a frequent symptom of the common cold is *malaise*. But why do people seem to get more colds during wintertime? Some blame it on the drop in temperature but weather has nothing to do with it. Instead, because sick people usually stay inside, it puts them in close range with other people who are seeking the warmth of indoors. Combine that with reduced air flow, and you get the conditions for colds to spread more easily than they do in warmer weather.

Spooky Words

These terrifying words will send a shiver down your spine.

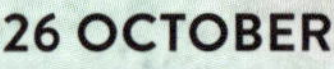

24 OCTOBER

Apparition

(ap-uh-RISH-uhn)

the unusual or unexpected sight of a person or thing, especially a ghost (noun)

Some visitors to the Tower of London claim to have seen the *apparition* of Anne Boleyn, the former Queen of England. According to legend, her ghost has been seen both with and without a head.

25 OCTOBER

Macabre

(muh-KAH-bruh)

involving death or violence in a way that is strange, frightening or unpleasant (adjective)

Archaeologists in Bulgaria made a *macabre* discovery when they dug up a skeleton from the 1200s with a stake through its chest. Experts believe that some early European cultures feared vampires and drove stakes through the hearts of the dead to prevent them from returning as the undead.

26 OCTOBER

Eerie

(EER-ee)

mysterious in a spooky or frightening way (adjective)

The National Film and Sound Archive in Canberra, Australia, is often called one of Australia's most haunted places. The building originally opened to the public in 1931 as the Institute of Anatomy and contained hundreds of skeletons and mummies. Today, staff members claim to hear *eerie* noises coming from areas of the building where dissection laboratories used to be.

27 OCTOBER

Hobgoblin

(HOB-gob-lin)

a small, mythical creature that creates mischief (noun)

In Welsh mythology, *hobgoblins* called 'the Bwbach' (BOO-bahk) are friendly, mischievous creatures who live with families and perform household chores in exchange for fresh cream. The term Bwbach means 'little scare' in Welsh because these hobgoblins are known for their pranks.

28 OCTOBER

Gruesome

(GROO-suhm)

causing horror or disgust (adjective)

In some Southeast Asian cultures, the *gruesome* ghost of a young woman's severed head haunts the countryside at night. According to legend, the severed head – called 'Krasue' in Thailand – flies through the night sky, painting the ground red with blood.

29 OCTOBER

Phantasm

(FAN-taz-uhm)

an illusion, apparition or ghost that is a figment of the imagination (noun)

Studies show that *phantasms* may just be a trick of the eye. People who are tired or performing mindless tasks often 'see' things out of the corner of their eye, but these things are actually our brains projecting random images.

30 OCTOBER

Establish

(ih-STAB-lish)

to successfully start or make something that did not exist before (verb)

Japan is home to many of the world's oldest businesses. Ichimonjiya Wasuke is a sweet shop in Kyoto that was *established* in the year 1000 CE. The shop is known for its history as well as its delicious rice cakes called aburi mochi that are believed to ward off sickness and evil.

31 OCTOBER

Top-notch

(TOP-noch)

extremely good; of the highest quality (adjective)

Within a year of coming out, Steven Spielberg's 1982 movie *E.T. the Extra-Terrestrial* had knocked *Star Wars* off the chart as the highest-grossing film of all time. The emotional story was inspired by Spielberg's own childhood and the imaginary alien friend he took comfort in when his parents divorced. It was one of the *top-notch* movies at the 55th Academy Awards, winning four Oscars, including Best Visual Effects.

Story of the Month

It was a night unlike any other at the haunted disco. At Club Bones, ***macabre apparitions*** danced with ***eerie hobgoblins*** to songs played ***fortissimo***. A ***crescendo*** in the music brought all the ghosts to the dance floor, where they bobbed and weaved to the ***staccato*** beats. Attendees danced, chatted and tumbled into one another in a show of ***slapstick*** fun. But the night soon turned from a ***schmoozing*** event into a confusing one!

Everything was going well until the volume went ***pianissimo***. Suddenly, the DJ booth ***ignited*** in sparks and the music cut out entirely. The whole place was sent ***topsy-turvy***, which ***altered*** the mood and brought on a serious ***malaise***. Then the creepy guests discovered that someone had ***mangled*** the cables to the DJ booth. The party turned into a ***whodunnit*** as guests tried to figure out who was responsible. The ***pugnacious*** mummies blamed the zombies for the interruption, while the ***cantankerous*** werewolves accused the vampires and ***vice versa***. A trio of witches, who had been performing ***acupuncture*** off to the side, threw down their needles and accused the trolls of the crime.

It was starting to look like something ***gruesome*** might happen. Then Detective Spectre stepped forwards. He was a ***scholar*** of mystery whose skill for remembering ghostly events ***derived*** from the use of ***mnemonics***. He ***established*** a theory. He pointed out that none of the haunted guests ate food, so the mice that lived in the walls of the disco were probably very hungry. The mice came out looking for dinner, saw the spaghetti-like cords and chomped away thinking they were ***edible***. Detective Spectre shone a light into the mouse hole to reveal three mice with fat bellies full of speaker wire. Mystery solved!

Meanwhile, someone had discovered a ***rickety*** cart in the closet along with an old boombox and a ***superfluous*** amount of music from Count Dracula's enormous song collection. Finally, as if the whole ordeal were merely a ***phantasm***, new tunes flowed from the boombox, the monsters floated back to the dance floor swept up by the ***legato*** music, and the party was once again ***top-notch***.

Nove

mber

1 NOVEMBER

Charisma

(kuh-RIZ-muh)

a special charm or appeal that causes people to feel attracted to and excited by someone (such as a politician) (noun)

Barack Obama, the first African-American US president, won over millions of voters with his *charisma* and drew record-breaking crowds to his rallies and inauguration. A powerful and inspiring public speaker, Obama's confident yet relaxed and respectful manner made him a hugely popular figure around the world. Although when he left the White House, one figure outshone him in the approval ratings: his wife, Michelle.

2 NOVEMBER

Buoyant

(BOY-uhnt)

capable of floating (adjective)

The Dead Sea, a lake in Israel, has up to nine times more salt than the world's oceans, making a person naturally *buoyant* in its waters. If you were to jump into the Dead Sea and lean back, your whole body would immediately pop up to the surface.

3 NOVEMBER

Aloof

•••••••

(uh-LOOF)

not involved with or friendly towards other people (adjective)

The 19th-century poet Emily Dickinson became famous only after her death. The *aloof* writer lived a reclusive life in her family's home where she wrote bundles of poetry and hundreds of letters in secret. When she died, her writings were discovered and published to much acclaim. She is now considered one of the great figures of American literature.

4 NOVEMBER

Erratic

(ih-RAT-ik)

acting, moving or changing in ways that are unexpected or unusual (adjective)

Cloudy with a Chance of Meatballs is a 2009 animated film based loosely on a much older picture book of the same name. Written by Judi Barrett, the 1978 children's story tells the tale of a town called Chewandswallow where the weather's timing is predictable – always at breakfast, lunch and dinner – but the elements are food instead of rain or wind. As the weather gets more *erratic*, the people of Chewandswallow are forced to deal with hamburger storms and mashed potato snow.

5 NOVEMBER

Medicinal

(mih-DISS-in-uhl)

having healing properties (adjective)

In the 1800s, an American doctor named John Cook Bennett started a tomato craze that swept the United States. Bennett claimed tomatoes had *medicinal* benefits so could cure a variety of ills. Tomato ketchup, which had only recently been invented, suddenly became the must-have drug – until consumers realised that its health benefits were wildly exaggerated.

6 NOVEMBER

Inherit

(in-HEH-rit)

to receive something from someone who had it previously (verb)

Humans get goosebumps because of a trait that was *inherited* from our animal ancestors. When animals are cold or feel threatened, tiny muscles make their hair stand up to keep them warm or make them look bigger to scare off potential attackers. Although modern humans no longer have the hairy bodies of our ancestors, our skin still stands up with goosebumps when we get cold or feel strong emotions such as excitement, anger or fear.

7 NOVEMBER

Palindrome

(PAL-in-drohm)

a word, verse, sentence or number that reads the same backwards or forwards (noun)

Try reading these *palindromes* from left to right, and then again from right to left:

- Was it a car or a cat I saw?
- Sit on a potato pan, Otis.
- Too bad I hid a boot.

8 NOVEMBER

Portable

(POR-tuh-buhl)

easy to move or carry around (adjective)

The invention of the audio cassette by Dutch engineer Lou Ottens in 1963 was quickly followed by the rise of the *portable* stereo player, also known as the boombox due to its ability to blast out sound. It was very popular among young urban communities during the 1970s and 1980s, especially those involved in hip hop culture. Sales of boomboxes declined when even smaller devices came along, like the Walkman.

9 NOVEMBER

Landlocked

(LAND-lokt)

surrounded by land (adjective)

Of all the *landlocked* countries in the world, only three of them are located entirely within another country's borders. Lesotho is a small country situated entirely within South Africa, while San Marino and Vatican City are both located within Italy.

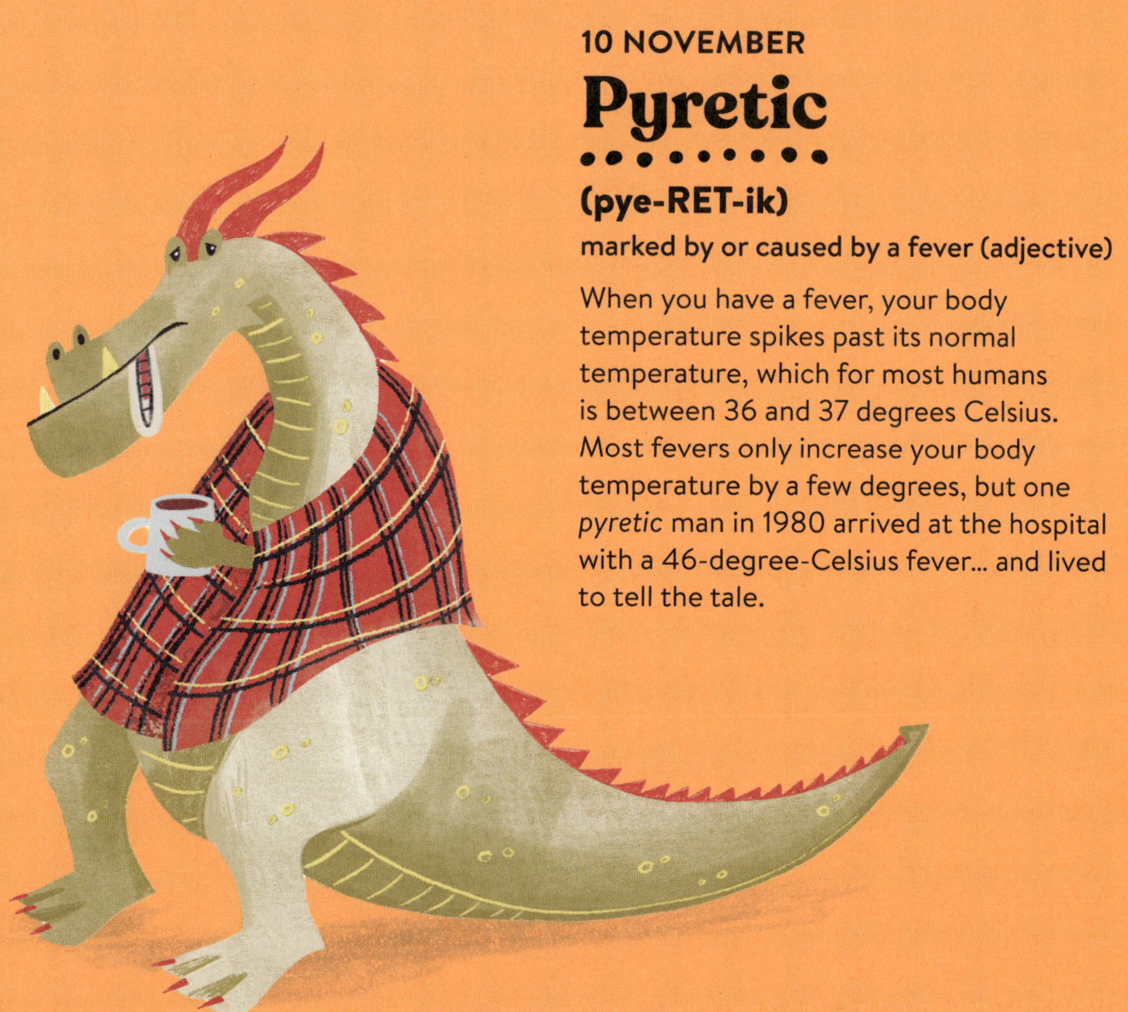

10 NOVEMBER

Pyretic

(pye-RET-ik)

marked by or caused by a fever (adjective)

When you have a fever, your body temperature spikes past its normal temperature, which for most humans is between 36 and 37 degrees Celsius. Most fevers only increase your body temperature by a few degrees, but one *pyretic* man in 1980 arrived at the hospital with a 46-degree-Celsius fever... and lived to tell the tale.

11 NOVEMBER

Pruritus

(proo-RYE-tuhss)

severe itching of the skin (noun)

Can you resist the urge to scratch an itch? It's a good idea to try, because scratching actually makes *pruritus* worse. But it can be almost impossible to resist the soothing sensation that scratching an itch creates in the brain... before the itch comes roaring back again.

12 NOVEMBER

Whippersnapper

(WIP-uh-snap-uh)

a young person who annoys older people by being very confident and acting like someone important (noun)

In an episode of *The Story of Tracy Beaker*, a children's television show inspired by Jacqueline Wilson's novel of the same name, Tracy marches into a football stadium and demands that the manager offer her friend Lol a trial. At first the manager is sceptical of the young *whippersnapper*, until Lol proves his skill by scoring a perfect goal.

Flowery Language

Take time to stop and smell these fragrant words, fresh from the garden.

13 NOVEMBER

Grevillea

(gruh-VIL-ee-uh)

a large genus of Australian shrubs and trees usually with showy orange and red flowers (noun)

Grevillea flowers bloom all year round, and are well suited to hot climates like Australia and New Guinea. Beetles, flies, bees and birds drink the flower's sweet nectar and help pollinate the plant throughout the year.

14 NOVEMBER

Thistle

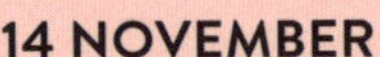

(THISS-uhl)

a prickly plant with large, tubular flowers (noun)

The *thistle* is the national flower of Scotland. The Most Ancient and Most Noble Order of the Thistle is an order of knighthood given to those who have made an outstanding contribution to Scottish culture.

15 NOVEMBER

Edelweiss

(AY-duhl-vyce)

a small mountain herb with dense, woolly white flowers (noun)

Edelweiss is native to the Alps in Europe. A stirring song called 'Edelweiss' appears in the movie musical *The Sound of Music*, which tells the tale of a family's escape from the Nazis during World War II.

16 NOVEMBER

Foxglove

(FOKS-gluv)

a tall plant that has many white or purple bell-shaped flowers growing on its stem (noun)

Foxglove is dangerous to eat, containing a chemical compound that can bring on confusion and change the perception of colour. Some art critics suspect that Vincent van Gogh's 'yellow period' – several years when the artist painted in yellow tones – was brought on by exposure to foxglove.

17 NOVEMBER

Dogwood

(DOG-wood)

a tree or shrub with clusters of small flowers, often with pink, white or red petals (noun)

Dogwoods are often planted in people's gardens for their beautiful flowers. But the tree is used for herbal medicine as well. For centuries people have used its bark and leaves to treat pain, fevers and dizziness.

18 NOVEMBER

Chrysanthemum

(krih-SANTH-uh-muhm)

a plant that has brightly coloured flowers and that is often grown in gardens (noun)

First cultivated in China, *chrysanthemums* were traditionally used as an edible herb in foods and teas. The flower quickly spread worldwide and was used in a wider variety of ways. In Japan, the flower was used on the emperor's official seal. In Europe, chrysanthemums are often brought to funerals.

19 NOVEMBER

Widget

(WIJ-iht)

any small mechanical or electronic device (noun)

In the 1980s, computer programs could only have one application open at a time. The team at Apple Computer, Inc. changed that. They created a program of simple tools, originally called 'desk ornaments', that required so little processing power they could run in the background of another program. A calculator, a clock, sticky notes and a puzzle game became the very first computer *widgets*.

20 NOVEMBER

Thermal

(THER-muhl)

of, relating to or caused by heat (adjective)

The Eiffel Tower in Paris was built to be able to sway in the wind, but the sun can also make it move. When the side that faces the sun heats up, it expands, causing the top of the tower to shift as far as 18 centimetres away from the sun. The 324-metre iron structure can also grow up to an additional 15 centimetres in height on warm days due to the same *thermal* expansion.

21 NOVEMBER

Harsh

(HAHRSH)

unpleasant and difficult to accept or experience (adjective)

Camels have three eyelids. Two of the eyelids have eyelashes that protect their eyes from the *harsh* blowing sands of the desert. The third eyelid, which moves from side to side, is much thinner and works to protect and clean off the eyes.

22 NOVEMBER

Caustic

(KAW-stik)

able to destroy or burn something by chemical action; very harsh (adjective)

Sodium hydroxide, a compound known primarily for its *caustic* properties, is used to manufacture everyday products like paper, soap, aluminium, cleaners and detergents. It is even used in food production for curing olives or browning Bavarian-style pretzels, giving them their characteristic crunch.

23 NOVEMBER

Moniker

(MON-ih-kuh)

a name or nickname (noun)

Born in 1942, Cassius Clay was one of the most famous boxers of all time. Shortly after winning the heavyweight world championship in 1964, he announced that he had converted to Islam and changed his *moniker* to Muhammad Ali. His refusal to fight in the Vietnam War saw him put on trial, but the courage he showed in standing up against the system made him an inspirational figure in the civil rights movement.

24 NOVEMBER

Concoction

(kon-KOK-shuhn)

something (such as a food or drink) that is made by mixing together different things (noun)

In 1905, an 11-year-old boy from California, USA, named Frank Epperson accidentally created a new *concoction* when he mixed water with a powdered soft drink flavouring and left it outside one cold night. The next day, he ate the frozen mixture off the wooden stirrer. Epperson called his discovery an 'Epsicle' and sold the first-ever ice lollies in his neighbourhood. He later changed the name to 'Popsicle'.

25 NOVEMBER

Pivotal

(PIV-uh-tuhl)

very important (adjective)

On 5 July 1996, Dolly the sheep was born. As the first cloned mammal ever to be created from an adult cell, her birth caused a worldwide sensation and was a *pivotal* moment in cloning technology. Dolly's existence proved that the cell of an adult mammal could be manipulated to produce an entirely new living mammal.

26 NOVEMBER

Parapet

(PAR-uh-puht)

a low wall at the edge of a platform, roof or bridge (noun)

Parapets might look decorative, but they have practical purposes. They first appeared on buildings across England after the Great Fire of London in 1666 because they slow the spread of fire between houses. Modern parapets on roofs are also designed to protect them from winds.

27 NOVEMBER

Kiosk

(KEE-osk)

a booth in a building or on the street where things (such as newspapers or tickets) are sold (noun)

Haines of Sloane Square is the oldest news *kiosk* in London, selling newspapers, drinks and more. Located a mile from Buckingham Palace, the business has been run by the same family ever since it opened in 1892. Princess Diana is rumoured to have been a regular customer as a teenager, stopping to flip through fashion magazines during the time she worked at a nursery school nearby.

28 NOVEMBER

Hobnob

(HOB-nob)

to spend time with someone (such as a famous or wealthy person) in a friendly way (verb)

Two con men were jailed after it was discovered they had tricked wealthy people out of more than 55 million euros. Using a silicone mask that made one of them look like the French defence minister, the men *hobnobbed* with politicians and business leaders over a video conference platform and asked them for money for government operations. The men approached more than 150 prominent people, including the King of Belgium.

29 NOVEMBER

Erupt

(ih-RUPT)

to become active or violent, especially suddenly (verb)

When Mount Vesuvius *erupted* almost 2,000 years ago, the ancient Roman city of Pompeii was buried in a thick layer of ash from the volcano. Archaeologists have since discovered a 'fast-food' counter there that served beef, pork, fish and snails to locals.

30 NOVEMBER

Harangue

(huh-RANG)

a forceful or angry speech (noun)

If you forget to finish your homework or crack jokes during class, your teacher may deliver a *harangue* about slacking off in school.

Story of the Month

Something was wrong with the queen. While she normally had the ***charisma*** to keep even the dullest conversation ***buoyant***, lately she was acting ***aloof*** and ***erratic***. Her weekly speeches from the top of the castle were normally lively and pleasant. But now, she began to ***erupt*** with ***harsh harangues*** from the ***parapets***. Her daughter, Cleona, ***hobnobbed*** with her mother and the royal elites of the ***landlocked*** kingdom enough to know that there was a problem. The ***pivotal*** moment came when the queen grew ***pyretic*** and could no longer speak. Her skin broke out in a rash and she experienced severe ***pruritus***. Try as they might, with their magic ***widgets*** and spells full of ***palindromes***, the court wizards could not fix the queen's ***thermal*** stress, nor her itchiness.

However, Cleona spent much of her time studying and knew that her mother's illness could not be cured with spells, but with something ***medicinal***. 'I can heal her! I just need some help!' Cleona exclaimed, but the royal court ignored her, calling her a ***whippersnapper***. Cleona knew that if her mother died it meant she would ***inherit*** the throne, but she did not want that to happen any time soon. The princess would save her mother, no matter what.

Cleona sneaked out of the castle and made her way to the nearby town. She wore plain clothes and used a false ***moniker*** to move about the market unnoticed. She found a ***portable kiosk*** selling many different types of plants. Cleona had made a list of what she needed – some mountain ***edelweiss***, desert ***grevillea***, leaf of ***dogwood***, ***chrysanthemum***, ***foxglove*** and a pinch of ***thistle***.

She greeted the travelling merchant and handed him the list. Cleona received the plants and raced back to the castle. She ground the plants down to a fine powder, mixed it with river water and rushed the ***concoction*** to her mother. The queen drank the ***caustic*** potion which burned as it went down her throat. Suddenly, the queen's fever broke. Long live the queen!

Dece

mber

1 DECEMBER

Skedaddle

(skih-DAD-uhl)

to depart quickly (verb)

When you're in danger or simply running late, you have to *skedaddle*. Famous skedaddlers include Cinderella, who had to dash home from the ball so fast she left behind a shoe, Luke Skywalker, who having fired upon the main reactor of the Death Star had to speed away before it exploded, and the White Rabbit in *Alice in Wonderland*, whose late arrival would have angered the Queen of Hearts and cost him his head.

2 DECEMBER

Descendant

(dih-SEN-duhnt)

a person, plant or animal related to an individual or group that lived at an earlier time (noun)

Rats can produce new litters of baby rats in only 21 days. If ideal conditions allow, then in three years, just two rats can theoretically produce half a billion *descendants*.

3 DECEMBER

Swarm

(SWORM)

a large number of living or non-living things grouped together, usually in motion (noun)

In some places, fireworks are being replaced by a large *swarm* of drones because drones are safer to operate. Thousands of drones are fitted with bright LED lights and controlled by a computer program that allows them to fly together to create colourful shapes and intricate patterns.

4 DECEMBER

Abominable

(uh-BOM-ih-nuh-buhl)

very bad or unpleasant (adjective)

Vlad the Impaler, or Vlad III Dracula, earned his fearsome reputation largely because of the *abominable* things he did to his enemies. This 15th-century Wallachian prince was so bloodthirsty that some think he may have partly inspired Bram Stoker's fictional Count Dracula.

5 DECEMBER

Satire

(SAT-yre)

humour that shows the weaknesses or bad qualities of a person, government, society, etc. (noun)

Practised throughout history, *satire* is a form of artistic expression that allows people to laugh at and understand different aspects of society. It can take many forms – novels, plays, films, TV shows, music and memes. Many places recognise the importance of poking fun at well-known leaders and institutions, and some countries, including Germany and Italy, even protect satire in their constitutions.

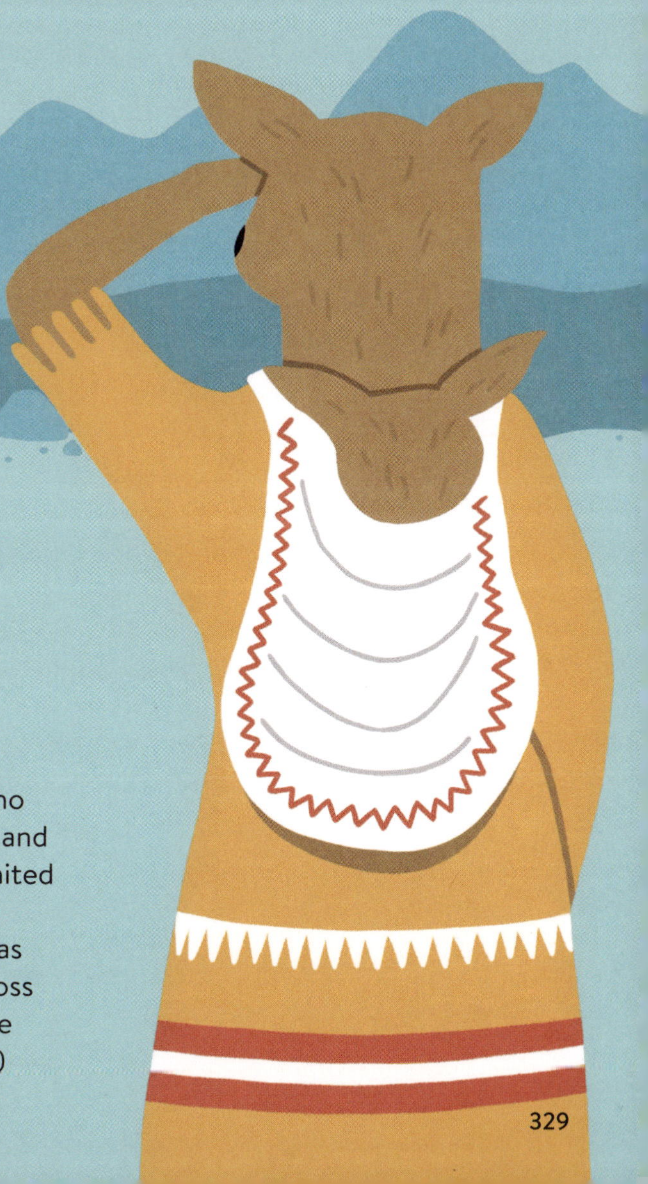

6 DECEMBER

Venture

(VEN-chuh)

to go somewhere that is unknown or dangerous (verb)

Sacagawea was a Native American woman who played a critical role in the 1804–1806 Lewis and Clark Expedition to explore lands that the United States had recently bought from France. The only woman in the group, Sacagawea served as an interpreter as the expedition *ventured* across the American West to the Pacific Ocean. (She carried her baby on her back the whole time.)

Wearable Words

These fashionable words never go out of style.

7 DECEMBER

Anorak

(AN-uh-rak)

a waterproof jacket, usually with a hood (noun)

The Inuit of Greenland make traditional *anoraks* from animal hides and treat them with fish oil to make them waterproof.

8 DECEMBER

Pince-nez

(panss-NAY)

a pair of glasses with a nose clip instead of arms and earpieces (noun)

During the American Civil War, eyeglass manufacturer John Jacob Bausch responded to metal shortages by creating a style of *pince-nez* made of rubber.

9 DECEMBER

Balaclava

(bal-uh-KLAH-vuh)

a warm hat that covers the head, neck and most of the face (noun)

During the Crimean War, British troops wore *balaclavas* to keep their face, head and ears warm in the bitter cold.

10 DECEMBER

Cummerbund

(KUM-uh-bund)

a wide piece of cloth (such as silk) that is worn around the waist beneath the jacket of a man who is formally dressed (noun)

The *cummerbund* originated in India and was traditionally worn by men. Today, it is commonly worn at formal events, often with tuxedos.

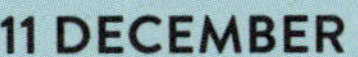

11 DECEMBER

Knickerbockers

(NIK-uh-bok-uhz)

loose-fitting short trousers that gather at the knee or calf (plural noun)

In the mid–1800s, *knickerbockers* were originally worn by men and boys, but they soon became popular with all sports enthusiasts. Because these trousers gathered at the knee, loose fabric couldn't trip athletes or get caught in bicycle spokes.

12 DECEMBER

Galoshes

(guh-LOSH-uhz)

tall rubber shoes that are worn over other shoes in wet weather to keep the feet dry (plural noun)

The Indigenous peoples of the Amazon region created *galoshes* centuries ago using sap from rubber trees. Historians aren't sure how they moulded the boots, but some believe these early inventors coated their feet with sap and held them over the fire until the sap hardened.

13 DECEMBER

Ruffian

(RUH-fee-uhn)

a brutal person; a bully (noun)

In an early episode of *The Simpsons* called 'Bart the General', Bart takes revenge on *ruffian* Nelson Muntz for all the beatings he's handed out. Taking military advice from his grandpa's friend, Bart trains an army of Nelson's other victims and declares war on the bully.

14 DECEMBER

Physically

(FIZ-ik-lee)

related to or involving the body or physical form (adverb)

The Australian Coat of Arms features images of a kangaroo and an emu that serve as symbols of the country's progress. Neither animal can *physically* move backwards easily. Besides being found only in Australia, the animals are thought to embody the Australian motto 'Advance Australia'.

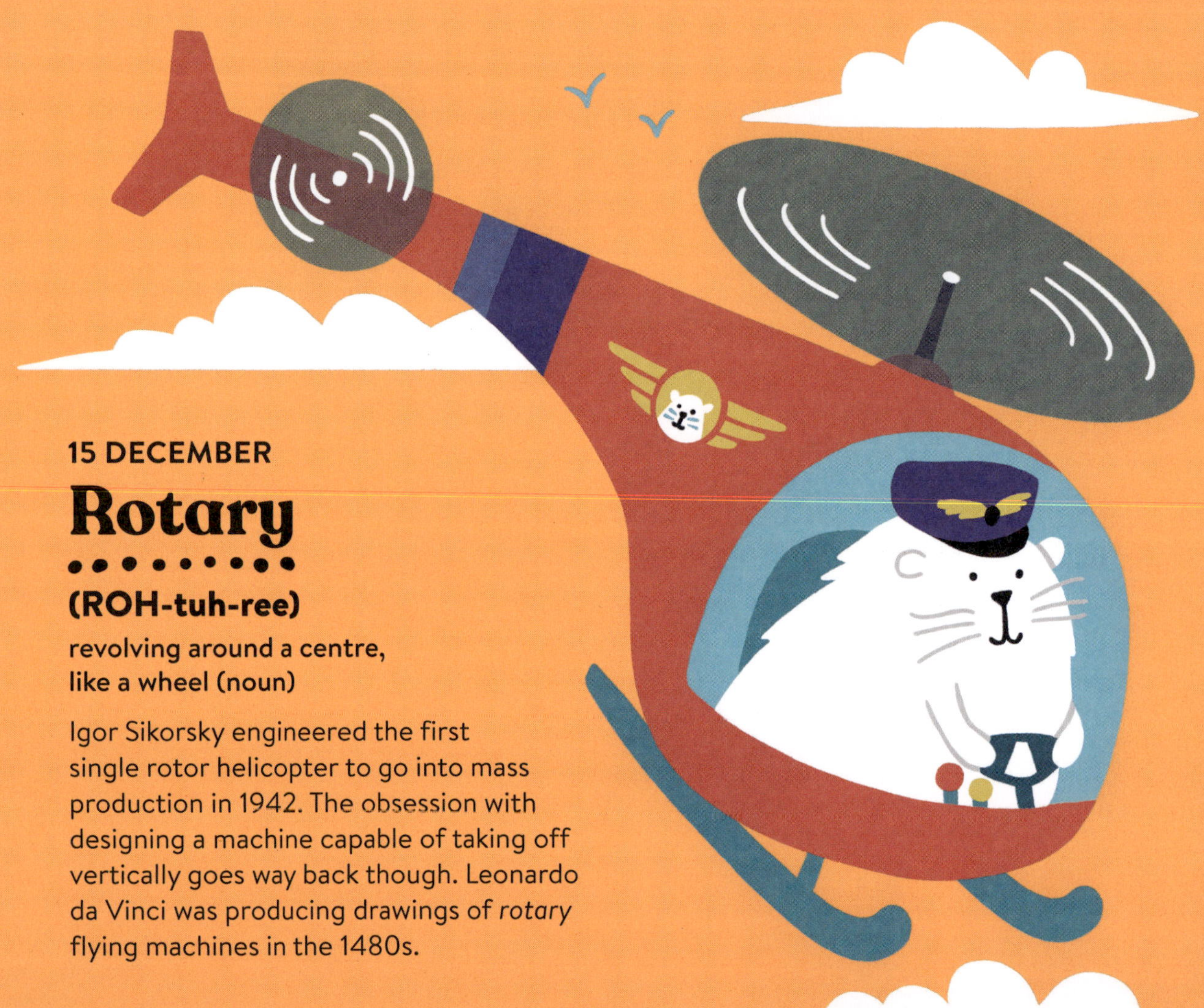

15 DECEMBER

Rotary

(ROH-tuh-ree)

revolving around a centre, like a wheel (noun)

Igor Sikorsky engineered the first single rotor helicopter to go into mass production in 1942. The obsession with designing a machine capable of taking off vertically goes way back though. Leonardo da Vinci was producing drawings of *rotary* flying machines in the 1480s.

16 DECEMBER

Aft

(AFT)

the back of a boat, ship or aeroplane (adjective)

On a ship, the terms *aft* and *stern* are often used interchangeably, but there is a difference. 'Aft' refers to the rearmost inside (or onboard) part of the ship, while 'stern' is the rearmost outside (or offboard) part of the vessel.

Our Daily Bread

Would bread by any other name taste as sweet? Absolutely.

17 DECEMBER

Naan

(NAHN)

an Indian bread that is round, flat and soft (noun)

Though *naan* has been around for thousands of years on the Indian subcontinent, the first written mention of the bread can be found in the writings of poet Amir Khusrau. According to his notes, naan was served in the 1300s at the Imperial Court in Delhi for elite members of society.

18 DECEMBER

Challah

(HAH-luh)

a bread made with eggs and typically braided or twisted before baking, traditionally eaten by Jewish people on the Sabbath and holidays (noun)

The size, shape and number of braids in a loaf of *challah* all have different meanings in the Jewish tradition. Often, the dough is braided to form twelve 'humps' that represent the twelve tribes of Israel.

19 DECEMBER

Brioche

(BREE-osh)

a soft and slightly sweet French bread, rich in butter and eggs (noun)

Queen Marie Antoinette of France is often quoted as the person who said, 'If they cannot eat bread, let them eat cake!', although there is no historical evidence for her saying this. What's more, the word she is supposed to have used is actually *brioche* rather than cake. Brioche, being rich in butter and eggs, and sometimes sweetened with sugar, is close to cake and was for centuries the food of the wealthy.

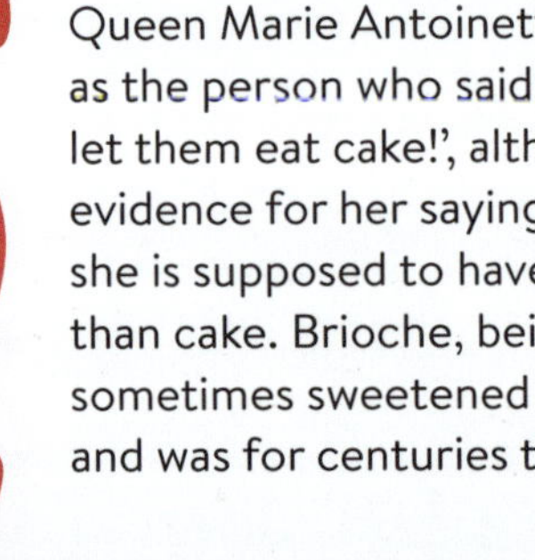

20 DECEMBER

Injera

(in-JAIR-uh)

a flat, spongy bread traditionally made from teff (noun)

Injera is made with the flour of an ancient grass called teff that is native to the eastern African countries of Ethiopia and Eritrea. The bread is cooked on a hot skillet and dotted with air bubbles.

21 DECEMBER

Lavash

(luh-VASH)

a large, thin flatbread with a rough surface caused by air bubbles (noun)

Lavash is an important bread in Armenian cuisine and plays a part in many cultural traditions. At Armenian weddings, lavash is often placed on the bride's shoulder to represent luck, wealth and new life.

22 DECEMBER

Focaccia

(fuh-KACH-ee-uh)

a flat Italian bread usually seasoned with herbs and olive oil (noun)

Different regions of Italy top their *focaccias* with different ingredients. In Liguria, focaccia is often topped with onions, green olives or anchovies. A sweeter taste can be found in Florence, where residents enjoy focaccia topped with grapes.

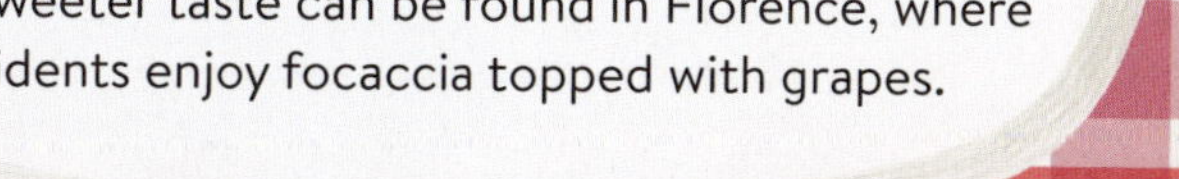

23 DECEMBER

Tradition

(truh-DISH-uhn)

a belief or custom handed down from one generation to another (noun)

In Thailand, people celebrate the Buddhist New Year (called Songkran) with a festival that is known as the largest water fight in the world. Throwing water is believed to wash away bad luck from the year before. While the *tradition* now often includes water guns, the holiday was originally celebrated with families coming together to pour water over statues of the Buddha.

24 DECEMBER

Caravan

(KA-ruh-van)

a group of people travelling together (noun)

The Silk Road was an ancient trade route that stretched from China all the way to Europe and parts of Africa. *Caravans* of travellers traded goods and products (not just silk) along the route, which helped spread various cultures, inventions and ideas across the vast area.

25 DECEMBER

Jocular

(JOK-yuh-luh)

jolly or fond of joking; humorous (adjective)

Comic Relief is a UK charity founded in 1985 in response to the famine in Ethiopia. Every two years, the charity puts on Red Nose Day, in which people everywhere are encouraged to do silly or funny things to raise money. There is also a televised fund-raising event in which comedians and celebrities come together to host an evening of *jocular* entertainment.

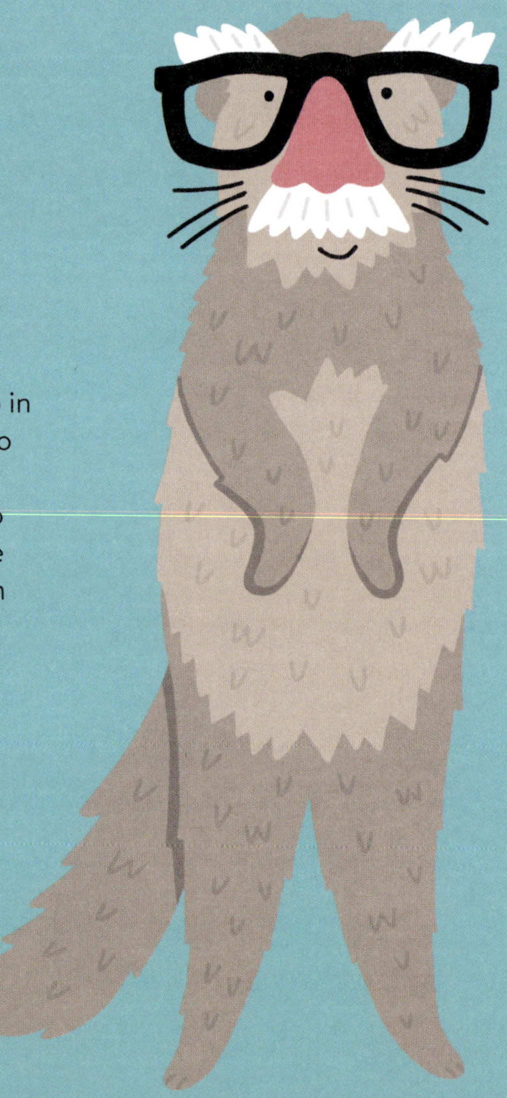

26 DECEMBER

Knick-knack

(NIK-nak)

a small trivial article usually intended as an ornament (noun)

The *knick-knack* salesman was a popular subject of Chinese court paintings. A 15th-century painting called 'The Knick-knack Peddler' shows a merchant with a cart selling trinkets, toys and sweet treats to children.

27 DECEMBER

Exorbitant

(ig-ZOR-bih-tuhnt)

going far beyond what is fair, reasonable or expected; too high or expensive (adjective)

While most dog collars are made of leather or nylon, some wealthy pet owners prefer a more *exorbitant* option like the Amour Amour Diamond Dog Collar, which costs £2.3 million. Adorned with 1,600 diamonds set in white gold, it is made of crocodile leather and is the most expensive dog collar in the world.

28 DECEMBER

Fluorescent

(fluh-RESS-uhnt)

able to give off visible light after being exposed to light, heat or another energy source (adjective)

In 2014, scientists found that some sharks can glow in the dark. The chain catshark and the swell shark use *fluorescent* green shapes in their skin to communicate with one another.

29 DECEMBER

Ballistics

(buh-LISS-tiks)

the science that studies the movement of objects (such as bullets or rockets) that are shot or forced to move forward through the air (plural noun)

Researchers in South Africa discovered 64,000-year-old 'stone points' in Sibudu Cave that are evidence of human-made arrows. The sharpened stones showed traces of blood and bone, proving that early humans had an understanding of primitive *ballistics* – they were able to launch arrows in the air and hit prey.

30 DECEMBER

Penultimate

(pih-NUL-tih-muht)

occurring immediately before the last one (adjective)

The Beatles' final live concert in August 1966 at Candlestick Park in San Francisco, USA, was technically their *penultimate* one. Thinking it would be their last show, musicians John Lennon and Paul McCartney brought cameras out onstage to take photos of the crowd and of themselves. However, their final show actually occurred in 1969 on the rooftop of the Apple Records building in London.

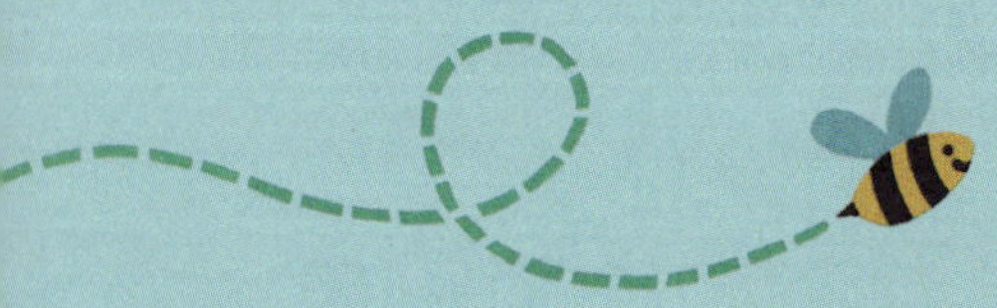

31 DECEMBER

Ebullient

(ih-BULL-yunt)

lively and enthusiastic (adjective)

In 2012 a South Korean pop song was released that took the world by storm. It was called 'Gangnam Style' and it brought K-Pop to a global audience. Its popularity can partly be put down to the *ebullient* moves of its singer, Psy, which triggered a 'horse dance' craze and saw the music video become the first ever to reach a billion views on YouTube.

Story of the Month

I have been lucky enough to live the life of an explorer. I've ***ventured*** across dusty lands and stormy seas to all corners of the globe. Along the way, I've learned valuable lessons. First lesson: approach challenging situations with a ***jocular*** attitude. This will allow you to make new friends wherever you go. I calmed a ***swarm*** of ***abominable ruffians*** in the desert by telling funny stories and trading ***knick-knacks***. One fellow even gave me a lesson in ***ballistics***, showing me his skills with a bow and arrow.

My second lesson: pack wisely so you don't spend an ***exorbitant*** amount of money on clothes. You will need outfits for all occasions. Standing at the ***aft*** deck of a ship gets cold, so if you want to catch a glimpse of the ***fluorescent*** jellyfish at night, you'll need to pack a warm ***anorak***, ***balaclava*** and a pair of ***galoshes***. But fancy invitations can come your way at any moment. I was once invited to sit with the ***descendants*** of royals at a concert hall and watch the premiere of a new ***satire***. Thankfully, I had packed my good pair of ***knickerbockers***, a ***cummerbund*** and my prescription ***pince-nez***.

My third lesson: respect and partake in local ***traditions***. I have encountered ***caravans*** of travellers on my adventures and celebrated their festivals, joined in their dances and dined on their food. Oh yes, I have broken many a bread in my day – ***focaccia***, ***naan***, ***challah***, ***brioche***, ***injera*** and ***lavash*** – and all were delicious.

Now that I am old, not ***physically*** what I once was, I am planning for my ***penultimate*** voyage. I am taking off in a new invention called a helicopter, which provides excellent views of the sky! I don't quite understand how it works but my crew assures me that this heavy ***rotary*** machine will fly. Please know that I am not sad, but rather ***ebullient*** to be taking my second to last trip. Now I must ***skedaddle*** and prepare for my departure. Maybe I'll learn some lessons along the way and take my final trip as an older but wiser adventurer.

Source Notes

This book's research process was multi-layered. The authors used a wide range of reliable sources for each topic, then fact checkers used additional sources to ensure each fact is correct. The result is more sources than there is room to share here. Below is a small sample of the authors' sources for each word.

Hoodwink: Lynch, Patrick. 'Catch Me If You Can: The Real Story of Frank Abagnale, Jr.', www.historycollection.com; ***Ovation***: 'Placido Domingo: Tenor of Our Times', www.cbsnews.com; ***Guffaw***: Ashish. 'Why Does Your Stomach Hurt When You Laugh Really Hard?', www.scienceabc.com; ***Epiphany***: Ballard, Elise. *Epiphany: True Stories of Sudden Insight to Inspire, Encourage, and Transform*. (New York, NY: Harmony Books, 2014); ***Ad-lib*** Nedd, Alexis. 'One of the Best Moments in *Infinity Wars* Was Completely Improvised', www.mashable.com; ***Klutz***: Selvin, Claire. 'Visitor Damages Antonio Canova Sculpture While Attempting to Take a Selfie', www.artnews.com; ***Mayhem***: 'International Pillow Fight Day', national-awareness-days.com; ***Fiasco***: McPherson, Angie. 'Slushy Sochi: Warm Weather Shows Challenges of Subtropical Snowmaking', www.nationalgeographic.com; ***Smithereens***: Mead, Thomas. 'Christchurch Family Restores Stained Glass Windows Shattered in Earthquakes', www.newshub.co.nz; ***Pandemonium***: 'Soaked Glastonbury Gets Under Way', www.bbc.com; ***Hazmat***: Than, Ker. 'Oil Spill Sullies Popular Tourist Beach in Thailand', www.nationalgeographic.com; ***Zany***: Raymond, Tom. 'Grock, Karl Adrien Wettach, Inducted into the Clown Hall of Fame in 1992', www.famousclowns.org; ***Rectify***: 'Spanish Fresco Restoration Botched by Amateur', www.bbc.co.uk; ***Cadre***: Morrison, Jim. 'The True Story of the Monuments Men', www.smithsonianmag.com; ***Dumbfounded***: Shapiro, Marc. *Lorde*. (London, UK: Omnibus Press, 2014); ***Tomfoolery***: Montgomery, L. M. (Lucy Maud). *Anne of Green Gables*. (New York, NY: Bantam Books, 1976); ***Virtuoso***: '100 Greatest Guitarists', www.rollingstone.com; ***Satchel***: Shakespeare, William. *As You Like It*. Edited by Barbara A. Mowat and Paul Werstine. (New York, NY: Simon & Schuster, 1997); ***Cantaloupe***: Lewis, Norman. *Word Power Made Easy*. (New York, NY: Anchor Books, 2014); ***Cheddar***: McLean, Rachel E. 'A Sharp Story: The Origin of Cheddar', www.culturecheesemag.com; ***Denim***: Plautz, Jason. '10 Places and the Words They Inspired', www.mentalfloss.com; ***Frankfurter***: 'Frankfurter', www.britannica.com; ***Satin***: 'Quanzhou', www.asiaculturaltravel.co.uk; ***Tuxedo***: Green, Dennis. 'We're Entering a Golden Age of Tuxedos – And These 8 Photos Show Why', www.businessinsider.com; ***Magnify***: 'First Magnifying Glass', www.guinnessworldrecords.com; ***Provoke***: 'War of Jenkins' Ear', www.britannica.com; ***Hubbub***: 'Falling Hare'. *Merrie Melodies*, by Bob Clampett, Warner Brothers, 1943; ***Marvel***: Lauer, Jonathon. 'The History of Marvel Comics', www.thenerdd.com; ***Fusspot***: 'The Browns and The Van Pelts: Siblings in Peanuts', www.schulzmuseum.org; ***Yelp***: 'Yelping in Dogs Can Be a Sign of Pain or Fear', www.canadianveterinarians.com; ***Potholing***: 'Everything You Need to Know About Caving', www.adventurebritain.com; ***Delusion***: Meares, Hadley. 'The Delusion That Made Nobles Think Their Bodies Were Made of Glass', www.history.com; ***Woebegone***: Mendoza Ph.D., Marilyn, A. 'Professional Mourning: An Ancient Tradition', www.psychologytoday.com; ***Grapple***: Nunley, Kim. 'Grappling vs. Wrestling', www.sportsrec.com; ***Punctual***: *Cinderella*. Directed by Clyde Geronimi, Wilfred Jackson and Hamilton Luske, Walt Disney Productions, 1950; ***Incorrigible***: Karetnick, Jen. 'Service Dogs 101 – Everything You Need to Know', www.akc.com; ***Oodles***: McLendon, Russell. 'Surprising Ways Animals Stock Up for Winter', www.treehugger.com; ***Sabotage***: Corera, Gordon. 'How Britain Pioneered Cable-cutting in World War I', www.bbc.com; ***Dilapidated***: 'Bodie State Historic Park', www.parks.ca.gov; ***Tandem***: Friend, Bonnie. 'The Romantic History of Tandem Cycling', www.welovecycling.com; ***Ailurophile***: Bridge, Mark. 'How Florence Nightingale Tended to a Hungry Mr Bismarck', www.thetimes.co.uk; ***Bibliophile***: Camuccini, Vincenzo. 'Ptolemy II Philadelphus Founds the Library of Alexandria', www.worldhistory.org; ***Cinephile***: 'The IMAX Difference', www.imaxmelbourne.com.au; ***Mycophile***: Petruzzello, Melissa. '7 of the World's Most Poisonous Mushrooms', www.britannica.com; ***Aplomb***: Branch, John. 'The Skateboarders Taking Over Are Among the Youngest Olympians in Tokyo', www.nytimes.com; ***Wanderlust***: Jerrard, Meg. 'Meet Audrey, The World's Most Well Traveled Woman', www.solofemaletravelers.club; ***Mastermind***: Charnas, Dan. 'The Rise and Fall of Hip-Hop's First Godmother: Sugar Hill Records' Sylvia Robinson', www.billboard.com; ***Docile***: Shelley, Mary Wollstonecraft. *Frankenstein, or, The Modern Prometheus: the 1818 Text*. (New York, NY: Oxford University Press, 1998); ***Collaborate***: Gagnon, Pauline. 'The Forgotten Life of Einstein's First Wife', www.scientificamerican.com; ***Chivvy***: 'The Technical Area', www.thefa.com; ***Bailiwick***: 'Kitchen Hierarchy – The Different Chef Titles Explained', www.morningadvertiser.co.uk; ***Glitch***: Moses, Asher. 'You Are Not Here: Apple Maps App Loses Users', www.smh.com.au; ***Impromptu***: Gallo, Carmine. 'How Martin Luther King Improvised "I Have A Dream"', www.forbes.com; ***Squeamish***: Kalter, Lindsay. 'Nerves of Steel, Shaky Stomachs', www.aamc.org; ***Quadrennial***: Wood, Stephen. '5 Things You May Not Know About Leap Day', www.history.com; ***Cahoots***: 'Great Train Robbery', www.britannica.com; ***Serendipitous***: McEvoy, Sophie. 'Riz Ahmed & Wife Fatima Farheen Mirza's Meet-Cute Is Straight Out Of A Rom-Com', www.bustle.com; ***Mishmash***: 'Mish Mash, Bulgarian Omelet', www.balkanfoodrecipes.com; ***Panache***: Williams, Keith. 'When New Yorkers Fell for a Singer They Had Never Heard', www.nytimes.com; ***Liberate***: Larosa, Brad. 'How Stefani Germanotta Became Lady Gaga', www.abcnews.go.com; ***Hoopla***: 'What Is Carnival Without You?', www.riocarnaval.org; ***Madcap***: St. Fleur, Nicholas. 'African American Heroes: Bessie Coleman', www.kids.nationalgeographic.com; ***Avuncular***: Travers, P.L. *Mary Poppins*. (Croydon, UK: HarperCollins, 2018); ***Jalopy***: www.rust2rome.com; ***Devour***: *Sesame Street*. Created by Joan Ganz Cooney and Lloyd Morrissett, Sesame Workshop, 1969–2016; ***Rendezvous***: 'Space Rendezvous', www.nasa.gov; ***Captivating***: Bruner, Raisa. 'The 10 Best Animal Instagram Accounts to Follow in 2019', www.time.com; ***Concentric***: 'Rulebook', www.worldarchery.sport; ***Peruse***: Vergano, Dan. 'Vatican Secret Archives Holds Tales Fascinating… And Not', www.usatoday.com; ***Blustery***: 'Fastest Wind Speed (Recorded by an Anemometer)', www.guinnessworldrecords.com; ***Balmy***: Zynda, Holly. 'Weather Loses Meaning at the Equator', www.weatherunderground.com; ***Cold snap***: Nace, Trevor. '"It's Almost Like Another Planet" – Coldest Temperature on Earth Recording in Antarctica', www.forbes.com; ***Scorcher***: 'Weather', www.nps.gov/deva; ***Cyclone***: Di Liberto, Tom. 'Tropical Cyclone Winston Causes Devastation in Fiji, A Tropical Paradise', www.climate.gov; ***Whiteout***: Van Pommeren, Rolph. 'Experience: I Almost Died in a Blizzard', www.theguardian.com; ***Swanky***: Lee, Nathaniel. 'Warren Buffett Lives in a Modest House That's Worth .001% of His Total Wealth', www.businessinsider.com; ***Zigzag***: 'Why Doesn't Lightning Travel in a Straight Line?', www.cbcradio.ca; ***Humdinger***: Carayol, Tumaini. 'Emma Raducanu: British 18-year-old Makes Tennis History With US Open Final Win', www.theguardian.com; ***Orderly***: Winterman, Denise. 'Queuing: Is it Really the British Way?', www.bbc.co.uk; ***Earworm***: Kraemer, David J. M., et al. 'Sound of Silence Activates Auditory Cortex', www.nature.com; ***Motley***: *The Wizard of Oz*. Directed by Victor Fleming and King Vidor, MGM, 1939; ***Mojo***: 'Martial Has Got his Mojo Back', www.skysports.com; ***Turbulent***: Thorpe, S.A. *An Introduction to Ocean Turbulence*. (New York, NY: Cambridge University Press, 2007); ***Escalate***: Carpenter, Megan. 'How the Escalator Forever Changed Our Sense of Space', www.smithsonianmag.com; ***Sputter***: 'Internal Combustion Engine Basics', www.energy.gov; ***Egad***: McCord, Carey P.M.D. 'Medically Adrift; How to Be Profane Politely – Minced Oaths'. Journal of Occupational and Environmental Medicine. Volume 65, Issue 5, May 2021; ***Brouhaha***: Barron, James. 'A Shell Is a Shell, No Matter Its Age', www.nytimes.com; ***Ludicrous***: 'How Do Funhouse Mirrors Work?', www.kingsheathmirrors.co.uk; ***Colossal***: Caryl-Sue. 'Big Blue', www.nationalgeographic.com; ***Aghast***: Longfellow, Henry Wadsworth. 'The Wreck of Hesperus'; ***Flummox***: 'What is Speedcubing?', www.rubiks.com; ***Trickle***: Halvorson, Todd. 'Astronaut with Flooded Helmet Felt Like Goldfish in Bowl', www.usatoday.com; ***Fawn***: Dotson, J. Dianne. 'How to Tell a Fawn's Age', www.sciencing.com; ***Cygnet***: 'Swan', www.britannica.com; ***Elver***: 'American Eel', www.fws.gov; ***Peachick***: 'Peacocks', www.nationalgeographic.com; ***Spat***: Lu, Connie. 'The Relationship Between Oyster Growing Cycle and Supply', www.pangeashellfish.com; ***Puffling***: 'Atlantic Puffin', www.kids.nationalgeographic.com; ***Nevertheless***: Resnick, Shawna K. 'Elizabeth I and the 1559 Act of Uniformity: A Study of the Impact of Gender Roles and Religious Conflict', www.nsuworks.nova.edu; ***Affable***: Sparkes, Ali. 'Top 10 Great Foxes in Children's Books', www.theguardian.com; ***Salinity***: 'Saline Water and Salinity', www.usgs.gov; ***Kibosh***: 'Champions League: Ash Alters Barcelona Travel Plans', www.bbc.co.uk; ***Jolt***: 'Electric Eel', kids.nationalgeographic.com; ***Roundabout***: 'What is a Roundabout?', www.wsdot.wa.gov; ***Waver***: Shepard, Julianne Escobedo. 'Meet FKA Twigs, Music's New Fashion Darling', www.thecut.com; ***Nil***: 'Nil by Mouth', www.macmillandictionary.com; ***Naught***: 'This Weekend's Boardmasters Festival 2019 Has Been Cancelled', www.kerrang.com; ***Diddly-squat***: Burke, Oliver. 'It Could've Been You', www.theguardian.com; ***Zilch***: Harrington, John et al. 'A Man Sues Himself? A Docket of 25 of the Weirdest, Silliest and Frivolous Lawsuits', www.usatoday.com; ***Dillydally***: 'Don't Dilly Dally', www.racingpost.com; ***Swagger***: 'Cowboy-style Walk Gives Burglar John Rigg Away', www.mirror.co.uk; ***Flibbertigibbet***: Greene, Harlan. 'Gertrude Legendre – The High Life to Spy Life, And Back', www.charlestonmag.com; ***Antenna***: 'Extreme Space Facts', www.nasa.gov; ***Wordy***: Kelly,

John. 'Oscars Acceptance Speeches Have Gotten Longer Over the Decades', www.abc7chicago.com; ***Verisimilitude***: Rowan, Jonathan Briche. 'True to Life: A Study of Lifelikeness in Fiction through Proust, Austen, Nabokov, and Joyce', University of California, Berkeley, 2014; ***Gargoyle***: Wells, Jeff, '10 Fearsome Facts about Gargoyles', www.mentalfloss.com; ***Axle***: 'Ten "Fun and Exciting" Facts About Engineering', www.nspe.org; ***Raconteur***: Andrew, Scottie. 'How a 'Hamilton' Song Helped Amanda Gorman Overcome a Speech Impediment', www.cnn.com; ***Retronym***: 'Penny-farthing History and Facts', www.bicyclehistory.net; ***Fossil***: Moskvitch, Katia. 'Ancient Giant Penguin Unearthed in Peru', www.bbc.com; ***Relic***: McSpadden, Kevin. '"Oscars of Chinese Archaeology" Reveals Top 10 Discoveries in China for 2020', www.scmp.com; ***Stratum***: Harris, Stephen L., 'Archaeology and Volcanism' in Sigurdsson, Haraldur, ed. *Encyclopedia of Volcanoes*. (Cambridge, MA: Academic Press Books, 1999); ***Excavate***: 'Rising Star Expedition', www.nationalgeographic.org; ***Artefact***: Learn, Joshua Rapp. 'Before the Inca Ruled South America, the Tiwanaku Left Their Mark on the Andes', www.smithsonianmag.com; ***Coprolite***: Prasad, Vandana et al. 'Dinosaur Coprolites and the Early Evolution of Grasses and Grazers'. Science Magazine, Nov. 2005, www.sciencemag.org; ***Beneficiary***: Hannah, Felicity. '10 of The Strangest Wills of All Time', www.theguardian.com; ***Uncouth***: Ness, Mari, 'She Doesn't Always Get Away: Goldilocks and the Three Bears', www.tor.com; ***Procrastinator***: Santella, Andrew. *Soon: An Overdue History of Procrastination, from Leonardo and Darwin to You and Me*. (New York, NY: Dey Street Books, 2018); ***Incognito***: Bushby, Helen. 'From Disguises to Bad Manners: How Celebs Avoid Being Pestered in Public', www.bbc.com; ***Jubilee***: 'Showa Memorial Park', www.japan-guide.com; ***Fuddy-duddy***: Apfel, Iris. *Iris Apfel: Accidental Icon*. (New York, NY: Harper Design, 2018); ***Sangfroid***: Ramaswamy, Chitra. 'Britain's First Female Firefighter: "There Was No Way I Was Going to Be the Weakest Link"', www.theguardian.com; ***Alias***: Cronin, Brian. 'TV Legends: Did Superman Actually Change in a Phone Booth on TV?', www.cbr.com; ***Castaway***: Mackling, Robert. *Castaway: The Extraordinary Survival of Narcisse Pelletier*. (Australia: Hachette Australia, 2019); ***Jetsam***: Thomson, Andrew. 'Artefacts Going Overboard', www.staugustinelighthouse.com; ***Salvage***: 'Ship Wrecks in the Cape Verdes', www.capeverdeinfo.org.uk; ***Flotsam***: Giaimo, Cara. 'What's the Most Surprising Thing You've Ever Found Washed Up on the Beach?', www.atlasobscura.com; ***Capsize***: Chen, Natasha. 'New Testimony Reveals What Happened Before the Golden Ray Capsized off the Georgia Coast', www.cnn.com; ***Contend***: 'Mary Fields', www.nps.gov; ***Skyrocket***: Vohra, Parth. 'Indian Movies Attract Millions Around the World – And That Number Looks Set to Grow', www.cnbc.com; ***Scoundrel***: Darby, Mary. 'In Ponzi We Trust', www.smithsonianmag.com; ***Defenestrate***: Artsy, Avishay. 'The Rock 'n' Roll Legacy of a Sunset Strip Hotel', www.kcrw.com; ***Befuddle***: Boyle, Alan. 'From Black Holes to Black History', www.nbcnews.com; ***Impetus***: 'Top 10 Chemical Reactions that You Can Repeat at Home', www.melscience.com; ***Kerfuffle***: Marland, Danny. '20 Years Ago Today, Wolves' Mascot Got Into A Scrap With Three Little Pigs', www.sportbible.com; ***Bamboozle***: 'Anansi', www.britannica.com; ***Domesticate***: Rutledge, Kim et al. 'Domestication', www.nationalgeographic.org; ***Exasperate***: Paez, Danny. 'How "Rage Quit" Became the Most Relatable Gamer Emotion', www.inverse.com; ***Ruse***: Aesop. *Aesop's Fables*. (New York, NY: Oxford University Press, 2002); ***Omnibus***: 'Word Count and Density', www.lotrproject.com; ***Pachyderm***: 'Top 10 Facts About Rhinos', www.wwf.org.uk; ***Septillion***: 'Myth Buster: No Two Snowflakes Are Alike? Very Likely, But It's Hard to Prove', www.reconnectwithnature.org; ***Rubberneck***: 'Dashcam Video Shows Multi-car Crash in Beaumont Caused by SpaceX launch', www.abc7.com; ***Doppelgänger***: Poe, Edgar Allen. *The Works of Edgar Allan Poe, The Raven Edition, Volume 2*. (New York, NY: P.F. Collier and Son, 1903); ***Cyborg***: Donahue, Michelle Z. 'How a Color-Blind Artist Became the World's First Cyborg', www.nationalgeographic.org; ***Android***: Hennessy, Michelle. 'Makers of Sophia the Robot Plan Mass Rollout Amid Pandemic', www.reuters.com; ***Debug***: Wall, Mike. 'A Glitch Nearly Killed NASA's Curiosity Rover After 6 Months on Mars', www.space.com; ***Automation***: 'How Will Automation Impact Jobs?', www.pwc.co.uk; ***Actuator***: 'The History of Automatic Doors', www.theautomaticdoorco.com; ***Prototype***: Newcomb, Alyssa. 'Google's Newest Self-Driving Car Prototype: A Look Inside', www.abcnews.go.com; ***Troubadour***: Thompson, Jonathan. 'Tracy Chapman: On Snakes, Faith and Busking for Food', www.independent.co.uk; ***Abhor***: Petruzzello, Melissa. 'Why Does Cilantro Taste Like Soap to Some People?', www.britannica.com; ***Recumbent***: Kaza, Roger. 'No. 2654 Bike Variations', www.uh.edu; ***Ecosystem***: '5 of the World's Most Mind Blowing Ecosystems', www.goodnet.org; ***Squeegee***: '2020 Speed Contest Rules', www.iwca.org; ***Harbinger***: Andrews, Evan. 'Eight Unusual Good Luck Charms', www.history.com; ***Curlicue***: 'Pig Info', www.pigspeace.org; ***Ponder***: Thoreau, Henry David. *Walden; or, Life in the Woods*. (New York, NY: Norton, 1992); ***Turbine***: 'Asbads (Windmill) of Iran', www.surfiran.com; ***Demolish***: Rodriguez, Juan. '4 Ways to Demolish a Building', www.thebalancesmb.com; ***Honorary***: Grundhauser, Eric. 'Bosco the Dog Mayor', www.atlasobscura.com; ***Pompadour***: Schneider, Martin. 'Retro Rockabilly Gangs of Tokyo', www.dangerousminds.net; ***Ephemeral***: 'Flowering Times and Duration', www.tcss.wildapricot.org; ***Intransigent***: Collinson, Alwyn. 'How Bazalgette Built London's First Super-sewer', www.museumoflondon.org.uk; ***Lavation***: Hernandez, Cathy. 'Buc-ee's Car Wash in Katy Gets Guinness Record as World's Longest', www.click2houston.com; ***Bugaboo***: Buddle, Chris. 'Why Are We So Afraid Of Spiders?', www.independent.co.uk; ***Animator***: Oppenheim, Maya. 'Veteran Studio Ghibli Animator Spirited Away at 77', www.independent.co.uk; ***Cosmetologist***: 'Madam C. J. Walker', www.history.com; ***Aviator***: 'Amelia Earhart', www.britannica.com; ***Haberdasher***: 'Company History', www.haberdashers.co.uk; ***Entrepreneur***: 'City of Los Altos History Resources Inventory', www.losaltosca.gov; ***Volcanologist***: Rowley, Dr Keith. 'How Being a Volcanologist Helped Me Deal with Pandemic', www.trinidadexpress.com; ***Heyday***: Vance, Jeffrey. *Chaplin: Genius Of The Cinema*. (New York, NY: Abrams Books, 2003); ***Mausoleum***: 'Mausoleum of the First Qin Emperor', www.unesco.org; ***Pizzazz***: 'Ten Incredible Elton John Performances', www.rollingstone.com; ***Nickelodeon***: 'This Londoner Has Been to the Same Cinema Every Week Since 1945', www.timeout.com; ***Hypothesis***: Semple, Kirk. 'Every Year, the Sky "Rains Fish". Explanations Vary.', www.nytimes.com; ***Marine***: 'Ocean', www.nationalgeographic.org; ***Panacea***: 'The History of Antibiotics', www.microbiologysociety.org; ***Loggerheads***: Wallisch, Pascal. 'Two Years Later, We Finally Know Why People Saw "The Dress" Differently', www.slate.com; ***Pulchritude***: Wilde, Oscar. *The Portrait of Dorian Gray*. (New York, NY: Penguin, 2003); ***Akimbo***: 'Swimming Syndrome', www.vetbook.org; ***Durian***: Ghosh, Prianka. '8 Things You Need To Know About Durian Fruit: The World's Smelliest Snack', www.theculturetrip.com; ***Tamarind***: Mertl-Millholen, Anne S. et al. 'Tamarind Tree Seed Dispersal by Ring-tailed Lemurs', www.pubmed.ncbi.nlm.nih.gov; ***Blackcurrant***: Hermiston, Roger. *All Behind You, Winston*. (London, UK: Aurum Press, 2016); ***Quandong***: Grant, Amy. 'Tips on Growing Quandong Fruit in Gardens', www.gardeningknowhow.com; ***Pitaya***: 'Dragon Fruit', www.agmrc.org; ***Opulent***: Meares, Hadley. 'How Versailles' Over-the-Top Opulence Drove the French to Revolt', www.history.com; ***Mulch***: '5 Surprising Facts About Mulch', www.westminsterlawn.com; ***Zeppelin***: Maksel, Rebecca. 'Docking on the Empire State Building', www.airspacemag.com; ***Minuscule***: Dell'Amore, Christine. 'World's Smallest Frog Found – Fly-Size Beast Is Tiniest Vertebrate', www.nationalgeographic.org; ***Karaoke***: Madrigal, Alexis C. 'Someone Had to Invent Karaoke – This Guy Did', www.theatlantic.com; ***Sprocket***: Raso, Michael. 'Sprocket Hole Photography', www.filmphotographyproject.com; ***Disperse***: 'Dispersion: The Rainbow and Prisms', www.lumenlearning.com; ***Taboo***: Blume, Judy. *Are You There God? It's Me, Margaret*. (New York, NY: Atheneum Books for Young Readers, 2001); ***Accumulate***: Cartwright, Mark. 'Mansa Musa I', www.worldhistory.org; ***Killjoy***: O'Neill, Therese. '5 of History's Biggest Killjoys', www.theweek.com; ***Monopoly***: Thorpe, JR. '7 Hilarious Corrupt Politicians From History', www.bustle.com; ***Ambidextrous***: '26 Celebrities Who Are Ambidextrous', www.ranker.com; ***Cicada***: Bradford, Alina. 'Facts About Cicadas', www.livescience.com; ***Botfly***: Lidz, Frank. 'I've Got Him Under My Skin', www.latimes.com; ***Katydid***: Williams, Sarah C. P., 'Why Katydids Sing in Unison', www.sciencemag.com; ***Millipede***: Morelle, Rebecca. 'World's Leggiest Millipede Put Under Microscope', www.bbc.com; ***Weevil***: 'Weevil: 9 General Types and How to Get Rid of Them', www.pestwiki.com; ***Mantis***: Hadley, Debbie. '10 Fascinating Praying Mantis Facts', www.thoughtco.com; ***Aardvark***: 'Factsheet Aardvark', www.ypte.org.uk; ***Odoriferous***: Daley, Jason. 'Scientists Played Music to Cheese as It Aged. Hip-Hop Produced the Funkiest Flavor', www.smithsonianmag.com; ***Igloo***: Holihan, Rich et al. 'How Warm is an Igloo?' Cornell University, 2003; ***Abacus***: 'Largest Abacus', www.guinnessworldrecords.com; ***Camouflage***: Jones, Benji. 'Chameleons' Craziest Color Changes Aren't for Camouflage', www.nationalgeographic.org; ***Odyssey***: Long, Tony. 'Nov. 14, 1889: Around the World in Only 72 Days', www.wired.com; ***Fortnight***: Ott, Michael. 'Pope Urban VII'. *The Catholic Encyclopedia*. (New York, NY: Robert Appleton Company, 1912); ***Chitchat***: Tolin, Lisa. 'Master Small Talk: Why You Need Chit-Chat in Your Life', www.nbcnews.com; ***Comeuppance***: Dahl, Roald. *The Twits*. (London UK: Jonathan Cape, 1980); ***Pareidolia***: McLendon, Russell. '14 Eerie "Faces" of Pareidolia from Nature', www.treehugger.com; ***Asteroid***: 'Hayabusa Spacecraft Returns Asteroid Artifacts From Space', www.nasa.gov; ***Gibbous***: 'Gibbous Moon', www.astronomy.swin.edu.au; ***Extraterrestrial***: ''Oumuamua', www.solarsystem.nasa.gov; ***Lunar***: Osborne, Hannah. 'Harrison Schmitt, the Last Man to Walk on the Moon, Was Allergic to Moon Dust – Warns Others May Be Too', www.newsweek.com; ***Nebula***: 'Helix Nebula – Unraveling at the Seams', www.nasa.gov; ***Supernova***: 'Supernovae', www.nationalgeographic.com; ***Deciduous***: '8 Interesting Facts About Autumn', www.metoffice.gov.uk; ***Phenomenon***: Gamillo, Elizabeth. 'Yosemite's "Firefall" Natural Wonder Illuminates El Capitan Through the End of February', www.smithsonianmag.com; ***Temerity***: Smith, Harrison. 'Kitty O'Neil, Deaf Daredevil Who Became "World's Fastest Woman", Dies at 72', www.washingtonpost.com; ***Cuckoo***: Stamp, Jimmy. 'The Past, Present, and Future of the Cuckoo Clock', www.smithsonianmag.com; ***Ostentatious***: McMah, Lauren. 'Inside the Insanely Decadent Life of the Sultan of Brunei', www.news.com.au; ***Trajectory***: Woodford, Chris. 'The Science of Sport', www.explainthatstuff.com; ***Unique***: Jeddy, Nadeem et al. 'Tongue

Prints in Biometric Authentication: A Pilot Study'. Journal of Oral and Maxillofacial Pathology, Jan–Apr. 2017; ***Regenerate***: 'Can You Live Without Your Liver?', www.upmc.com; ***Cornucopia***: Grundhauser, Eric. 'From Zeus to Williams-Sonoma: The History of the Cornucopia', www.atlasobscura.com; ***Quid pro quo***: 'Chimpanzee Habitat', www.conservenature.org; ***Juggernaut***: 'Great Hurricane of 1780', www.britannica.com; ***Agenda***: Andrews, Evan. '8 Historical Figures with Unusual Work Habits', www.history.com; ***Crochet***: Salomone, Andrew. 'Yarn-Bombing Artist Sets Out to Crochet Across The USA', www.vice.com; ***Adjacent***: Daley, Jason. 'Archaeologists Uncover an Ancient Roman Game Board at Hadrian's Wall', www.smithsonianmag.com; ***Cerulean***: Larson, Anna G. et al. 'Pantone's Colors of the Year Represent a Changing World', www.duluthnewstribune.com; ***Puce***: Challamel, Augustin. *The History of Fashion In France: Or The Dress Of Women From The Gallo-Roman Period To The Present Time*. (Washington, D.C.: Westphalia Press, 2018); ***Flaxen***: Dickens, Charles. *David Copperfield*. (New York, NY: Modern Library, 2000); ***Cyan***: 'CMYK', www.techterms.com; ***Periwinkle***: Braid, Fara. 'Lapis Lazuli Symbolism', www.gemsociety.org; ***Chartreuse***: Kelleher, Katy. 'Chartreuse, the Color of Elixirs, Flappers, and Alternate Realities', www.theparisreview.org; ***Dilute***: Little, Becky. 'When London Faced a Pandemic – And a Devastating Fire', www.history.com; ***Tittle-tattle***: Linder, Douglas. 'The Witchcraft Trials in Salem: A Commentary', www.umkc.edu; ***Contentious***: Niiler, Eric. 'Soccer Is Getting Slower and More Fair – and That's a Problem', www.wired.com; ***Inflation***: Jones, Paul Anthony. 'Hyperinflation Gone Mad: When German Children Made Kites From Money', www.mentalfloss.com; ***Perspire***: Phillips, Quinn. 'When It Comes to Sweat, What's Considered Normal?' www.everydayhealth.com; ***Predict***: Breitman, Daniela. 'Today In Science: Discovery Of Neptune', www.earthsky.org; ***Juxtapose***: Zielinski, Sarah. 'Comparing Apples and Oranges', www.smithsonianmag.com; ***Rustic***: Clapp, Susannah. 'How Tove Jansson's Love of Nature Shaped the World of the Moomins', www.theguardian.com; ***Spurn***: Shakespeare, William, *Romeo and Juliet*. Edited by René Weis (London, UK: The Arden Shakespeare, 2012); ***Kerplunk***: Nix, Elizabeth. 'Did an Apple Really Fall on Isaac Newton's Head?', www.history.com; ***Conclave***: 'Hermetic Order of the Golden Dawn', www.newworldencyclopedia.org; ***Ignite***: 'How Car Engines Work: Lesson for Kids', www.study.com; ***Acupuncture***: 'Acupuncture', www.mayoclinic.org; ***Vice versa***: Cohen, Jennie. '8 Legendary Duels', www.history.com; ***Slapstick***: 'Laurel and Hardy', www.britishclassiccomedy.co.uk; ***Schmooze***: Avery, Dan. 'This Artist Faked Being a Billionaire to Photograph New York City's Best Views', www.architecturaldigest.com; ***Alter***: Dixon, Emily. 'Here's How Princess Beatrice Altered One of the Queen's Favorite Dresses for Her Wedding', www.marieclaire.com; ***Musical Words***: 'Dynamics', www.phoenixsymphony.org; ***Superfluous***: 'Great Pacific Garbage Patch', www.nationalgeographic.org; ***Mangle***: 'Barnett Newman', www.stedelijk.nl; ***Scholar***: 'Science and Technology in Medieval Islam', www.mhs.ox.ac.uk; ***Whodunnit***: '10 Facts About Agatha Christie Fans Should Know', www.southernliving.com; ***Topsy-turvy***: Hirst, K. Kris. 'The Dust Veil Environmental Disaster of AD 536', www.thoughtco.com; ***Derive***: Alfaro, Danilo. 'What Are Marshmallows Made Of?' www.thespruceeats.com; ***Pugnacious***: Cohen, Patricia. 'Reason Seen More as Weapon Than Path to Truth', www.nytimes.com; ***Cantankerous***: Cisneros, Sandra. *Caramelo*. (London, UK: Bloomsbury, 2003); ***Rickety***: 'Louvre to Exhibit Balintore Shed Door Marble Bust', www.bbc.com; ***Edible***: Gelling, Natasha. 'The Science Behind Honey's Eternal Shelf Life', www.smithsonianmag.com; ***Malaise***: Kaulessar, Ricardo. 'Can You Actually Get Sick From the Weather Changing?' www.northjersey.com; ***Apparition***: Young, Nick. 'Who Exactly Are The Ghosts Of London?' www.londonist.com; ***Eerie***: Travers, Penny. 'National Film and Sound Archive One of Australia's "Most Haunted Buildings"', www.abc.net.au; ***Macabre***: Nuwer, Rachel. '"Vampire Grave" in Bulgaria Holds a Skeleton With a Stake Through Its Heart', www.smithsonianmag.com; ***Hobgoblin***: 'The Meaning of Bwbach Explained', www.bluestonewales.com; ***Gruesome***: Shum, Sharon. 'Krasue is the Girl with Serious Detachment Issues', www.vice.com; ***Phantasm***: Mapes, Diane. 'Have You Seen a Ghost? There May Be a Medical Reason', www.today.com; ***Establish***: Pinsker, Joe. 'Japan's Oldest Businesses Have Survived for More Than 1,000 Years', www.theatlantic.com; ***Top-notch***: Hutchinson, Sean. '20 Amazing Facts About E.T. the Extra-Terrestrial', www.mentalfloss.com; ***Charisma***: Oppenheim, Maya. 'Michelle Obama Named "Most Admired" Woman in the World in US Survey', www.independent.co.uk; ***Buoyant***: Colby, Terri. 'Living it up in the Dead Sea', www.chicagotribune.com; ***Aloof***: 'Emily Dickinson', www.biography.com; ***Erratic***: Barrett, Judi. *Cloudy With a Chance of Meatballs*. (New York, NY: Aladdin Paperbacks, 1982); ***Medicinal***: Smith, Andrew F. 'Tomato Pills Will Cure All Your Ills'. Pharmacy in History, 1991; ***Inherit***: Bubenik, George A. 'Why Do Humans Get "Goosebumps" When They Are Cold, or Under Other Circumstances?', www.scientificamerican.com; ***Portable***: Carlson, Michael. 'Lou Ottens Obituary', www.theguardian.com; ***Landlocked***: Dempsey, Caitlin. 'Landlocked Countries', www.geographyrealm.com; ***Pyretic***: Klibanoff, Eleanor. 'You Might Be Surprised When You Take Your Temperature', www.npr.org; ***Pruritus***: 'Itchy Skin (Pruritus)', www.mayoclinic.org; ***Whippersnapper***: 'Football Trial'. *The Story of Tracy Beaker*, directed by Joss Agnew, written by Jacqueline Wilson (book) and Andrew Walker, season 3, episode 17, British Broadcasting Corporation, 2004; ***Grevillea***: 'Seed Notes for Western Australia', www.dpaw.wa.gov.au; ***Chrysanthemum***: 'History of the Chrysanthemum', www.mums.org; ***Foxglove***: 'The Incredible Tale of the Foxglove, from Curing to Disease to Inspiring Van Gogh's Most Striking Paintings', www.countrylife.co.uk; ***Edelweiss***: *The Sound of Music*. Directed by Robert Wise, 20th Century Fox, 1965; ***Dogwood***: Bartons, Siobhan. 'All About The Flowering Dogwood', www.thetreecenter.com; ***Thistle***: 'About Scotland's National Flowers', www.visitscotland.com; ***Widget***: Lowensohn, Josh. 'A Brief History of Widgets', www.theverge.com; ***Thermal***: Palermo, Elizabeth. 'Eiffel Tower: Information & Facts', www.livescience.com; ***Harsh***: Hiskey, Daven. 'Camels Have Three Eyelids', www.todayifoundout.com; ***Caustic***: 'Sodium Hydroxide', www.chemicalsafetyfacts.org; ***Moniker***: Hauser, Thomas. 'Muhammad Ali', www.britannica.com; ***Concoction***: Pope, Shelby. 'How An 11-Year-Old Boy Invented The Popsicle', www.npr.org; ***Pivotal***: Weintraub, Karen. '20 Years After Dolly the Sheep Led the Way – Where Is Cloning Now?', www.scientificamerican.com; ***Parapet***: 'The Origin of The Parapet', www.iroofing.org; ***Kiosk***: Goldstein, Danielle. 'Meet the Man (And His Mum) Running London's Oldest Newstand: Haines of Sloane Square', www.timeout.com; ***Hobnob***: 'Le Drian Case: Fraudsters Who Wore Mask of French Minister Jailed', www.bbc.com; ***Erupt***: 'Pompeii: Ancient "Fast Food" Counter to Open to the Public', www.bbc.com; ***Skedaddle***: *Star Wars: A New Hope (Episode IV)*. Directed by George Lucas, Lucasfilm with Twentieth Century-Fox Film Corporation, 1977; ***Descendant***: 'How Quickly Rats Can Breed is Terrifying', www.qsrmagazine.com; ***Swarm***: GrrlScientist. 'Drone Light Shows "Way Cooler" Than Fireworks', www.forbes.com; ***Abominable***: Pallardy, Richard. 'Vlad the Impaler', www.britannica.com; ***Satire***: Geisler, Michael E. *National Symbols, Fractured Identities: Contesting the National Narrative*. (Lebanon, NH: University Press of New England, 2005); ***Venture***: 'Sacagawea', www.biography.com; ***Anorak***: 'Anorak', www.macmillandictionaryblog.com; ***Pince-nez***: 'Hindsight Is 20/20: The Pince-Nez', www.2020mag.com; ***Balaclava***: Hartston, William. 'Top 10 Facts About the Crimean War', www.express.co.uk; ***Cummerbund***: 'Cummerbund', www.britannica.com; ***Knickerbockers***: Newman, Alex. *Fashion A to Z: An Illustrated Dictionary*. (London, UK: Laurence King Publishing Ltd., 2012). ***Galoshes***: Peeples, Lynne. 'The Origin of Rubber Boots', www.scientificamerican.com; ***Ruffian***: 'Bart the General'. *The Simpsons*, created by Matt Groening, season 1, episode 5, Fox Broadcasting Company, 1990; ***Physically***: 'Commonwealth Coat of Arms', www.pmc.gov.au; ***Rotary***: 'Leonardo da Vinci's Helicopter: 15th-century Flight of Fancy Led to Modern Aeronautics', www.theconversation.com; ***Aft***: '15 Basic Boat Terms', www.wavesboatclub.com; ***Naan***: Dash, Madhulika. 'Food Story: How Naan and Kulcha Became India's Much-loved Breads', www.indianexpress.com; ***Challah***: 'The Significance of Challah', www.modernistbread.com; ***Brioche***: Cunningham, John M. 'Did Marie-Antoinette Really Say "Let Them Eat Cake"?', www.britannica.com; ***Injera***: Liu, Karon. 'Ethiopian Injera a Tradition that Spans Thousands of Years', www.thestar.com; ***Lavash***: Leahy, Kate. 'On the Lavash Trail in Armenia', www.smithsonianmag.com; ***Focaccia***: Baldwin, Eleonora. 'A Brief History of Focaccia', www.theamericanmag.com; ***Tradition***: 'Songkran: Thailand Celebrates Buddhist New Year with Water Fights', www.bbc.com; ***Caravan***: 'Caravanserai', www.nationalgeographic.org; ***Jocular***: 'A Night of Comic Relief', www.bbc.com; ***Knick-knack***: 'Knickknack Peddler, 13th–15th Century', www.metmuseum.org; ***Exorbitant***: Desai, Yash. 'La Collection de Bijoux: The Most Expensive Dog Diamonds', www.businessinsider.com; ***Fluorescent***: Signorelli, Laura. 'Ten Interesting Facts About Sharks', www.sea.museum; ***Ballistics***: Gill, Victoria. 'Oldest Evidence of Arrows Found', www.bbc.com; ***Penultimate***: 'Live: Candlestick Park, San Francisco: The Beatles' Final Concert', www.beatlesbible.com; ***Ebullient***: Chung, Gigi. 'The 10 Most Popular K-Pop Artists and Bands', www.theculturetrip.com.

Illustrations

Josy Bloggs
Pgs 8, 20, 40, 43, 46, 48, 51–52, 53, 55, 60–61, 67, 68, 70–71, 80–81, 84, 100, 107, 111, 113, 125, 127, 128, 130–31, 132, 138, 161, 165, 169, 176–77, 180, 182–83, 186–87, 190, 193, 194, 200, 203, 208–09, 213, 216, 219, 220, 223, 224, 229, 243, 244, 246, 251, 253, 254, 257, 258, 261, 267, 268, 272–73, 275, 289, 290–91, 299, 313, 336–37, 341, 343, 348–49

Emily Cox
Pgs 6, 13, 36, 42, 44, 46–47, 54, 58–59, 66, 74, 79, 87, 90–91, 96, 98, 103, 104–05, 106, 133, 137, 142, 143, 144, 150, 155, 156, 159, 160, 166, 171, 172, 175, 188, 191, 192, 195, 196–97, 198–99, 201, 202, 211, 214–15, 217, 218, 221, 222, 226–27, 228, 236, 240, 242, 245, 247, 252, 266, 279, 284, 286–87, 295, 302, 306–07, 310, 326, 328, 330–31

James Gibbs
Pgs 9, 14–15, 16–17, 18, 21, 22, 27, 28, 35, 39, 49, 50, 56, 65, 76–77, 83, 88–89, 95, 99, 101, 108, 110, 117, 118–19, 129, 146–47, 153, 162–63, 164, 167, 174, 189, 210, 237, 239, 248–49, 262–63, 270, 274, 276–77, 278, 282, 285, 288, 294, 297, 300–01, 305, 308, 311, 312, 314–15, 316–17, 319, 324, 327, 329, 332, 334–35, 340, 342, 344–45

Liz Kay
Pgs 7, 10–11, 12, 19, 23, 24–25, 26, 29, 30–31, 34, 37, 38, 41, 57, 64, 69, 72–73, 75, 78, 82, 85, 86, 94, 97, 102, 109, 112, 114–15, 116, 122–23, 124, 126, 134–35, 136, 139, 140–41, 145, 151, 152, 154, 157, 158, 168, 170, 173, 181, 184–85, 204–05, 212, 225, 230–31, 232–33, 238, 241, 250, 255, 256, 259, 260, 269, 271, 280–81, 283, 296, 298, 303, 304, 309, 318, 320–21, 325, 333, 338, 339, 346–47